Contracts as Reinvented Institutions in the Public Sector: A Cross-Cultural Comparison

Contracts as Reinvented Institutions in the Public Sector: A Cross-Cultural Comparison

Carsten Greve and Niels Ejersbo

Westport, Connecticut
London

Library of Congress Cataloging-in-Publication Data

Greve, Carsten.
    Contracts as reinvented institutions in the public sector : a cross-cultural
comparison / Carsten Greve and Niels Ejersbo.
        p. cm.
    Includes bibliographical references and index.
    ISBN 1–56720–528–3 (alk. paper)
    1. Public contracts.   2. Public contracts—Cross-cultural studies.   3. Contracting out.
    4. Contracting out—Cross-cultural studies.   I. Ejersbo, Niels.   II. Title.
        HD3860.G74   2005
        352.5'3—dc22   2004011895

British Library Cataloguing in Publication Data is available.

Library of Congress Catalog Card Number: 2004011895
ISBN: 1–56720–528–3

First published in 2005

Praeger Publishers, 88 Post Road West, Westport, CT 06881
An imprint of Greenwood Publishing Group, Inc.
www.praeger.com

Printed in the United States of America

The paper used in this book complies with the
Permanent Paper Standard issued by the National
Information Standards Organization (Z39.48–1984).

10   9   8   7   6   5   4   3   2   1

Contents

Tables and Figures

TABLES

FIGURES

Preface and Acknowledgments

Contracting has become a worldwide phenomenon. We wanted to write a book about how contracting is practiced and understood in different parts of the world. This book is the central publication from our four-year research project on "the public sector on contract." Studying it from a public governance and management perspective has been an immensely interesting and satisfying process.

We deliberately chose the term "contracting" instead of "privatization" or "contracting out." Both those terms have come to mean so much to so many people. Instead we wanted to look at the contracting process and the institutions that surround that process. Contracting, in our understanding, involves both contracting inside the public sector and contracting between public purchasers and private providers of public services. Understanding the contracting process in two different institutional settings such as the United States and Scandinavia has been a huge challenge to us. Whether the effort brings new insights to the contracting process is up to you, the readers, to decide.

Several of the book's chapters have been presented as papers for scientific conferences around the world. We have presented our work at conferences by the European Group of Public Administration (EGPA), the International Research Symposium on Public Management (IRSPM), and the American Society for Public Administration (ASPA) and at the Nordic Local Government Research Conference and would like to thank all participants in our sessions for their comments and criticisms.

In writing this book we have incurred many debts, and we will try to extend our thanks to the people and organizations that helped make the book and the research project come to life. We would like to thank Lawrence Martin, Gavin Drewry, Thierry Tanqurel, Karin Bryntse, Graeme Hodge, Seok Hwan Lee and Oliver James, who helped with suggestions and comments in various ways, Donald F. Kettl for providing an opportunity for a research stay at the University of Wisconsin-Madison, Local Government Denmark ("Kommunernes Landsforening") for cooperation on the survey of Danish local governments, the people we interviewed in Madison, Wisconsin, and Odense, Denmark, our research assistants Mette Bjørn-Andersen, Mette Fogh, and Katrine Pondal, the students from our graduate courses on contracts in the public sector, colleagues at the University of Southern Denmark and University of Copenhagen, and the Danish Social Science Research Council for providing the research grant in 2000.

Praeger has been supportive and incredibly patient with us all the way through: Hillary Claggett, who took on the project; Nick Phillipson, who continued the process; his assistant Brien McDonald; and everybody else at Praeger who has helped with the manuscript.

Finally, we want to extend our deepest and heartfelt thanks to both our families, who were there for us all the time. You wondered what your husbands and daddies were working on long way from home at conferences in faraway places, and this book is the answer. Thanks for all your patience and support.

Niels Ejersbo and Carsten Greve

Introduction: Contracting on the Policy Agenda

Contracting can be understood as "the design and implementation of contractual relations between purchasers and suppliers" (Domberger 1998, 12). A contract can be defined as "an agreement between two or more persons intended to create a legal obligation between them and to be legally enforceable" (Drewry 2000, 257). "Contracting out will be used to refer to a situation where publicly funded services are purchased from private organizations" (Boston 1995, 82). "To hire an external organization to provide goods or services rather than provide it in-house" (Domberger 1998, 210). "Privatization is the transfer of assets and/or service functions from public to private hands. It includes therefore activities that range from selling State Owned Enterprises to contracting out public services with private contractors" (Hodge 2000, 14, quoting from Leiberman 1993).

In recent years contracting has been used both within the limits of the public sector and between a public purchaser and a private provider. When a public purchaser buys a product or a service from a private provider, the matter is referred to as "contracting out." In recent years, public sector organizations have also taken up contracts as governing and management tools to boost their own performances. When a public body "buys" a product or a service in-house from a public body provider, we refer to the matter as "performance contracting" (also known in some places as "internal contracting," as opposed to "external contracting"). A performance contract within the borders of the public sector will typically not create any legal obligation.

In today's public sector contracting has caught on as a governance mechanism for sharing power between the public and the private sectors (Kettl 1993). Behn and Kant (1999, 479) note that "contracting out is in. All sorts of governments are contracting for all kinds of goods and services." Contracting for public services is part of a wider privatization movement that has swept the world during the last twenty-five years (Savas 2000). Contracting has been an integrated part of the New Public Management movement that has influenced public sector reform in most OECD countries (Hood 1991; Fortin and van Hassel, eds., 2000). Privatization is a term that also encompasses the sale of government enterprises, voucher schemes, and other measures. In this book, we will use the term *contracting*, as specified above, instead of the wider term "privatization."

Contracting out is also going on in the private sector, where it is more commonly known as "outsourcing," but the decision of whether "to make or buy" is essentially the same (Domberger 1998). The private sector has been outsourcing its IT-functions for a long time, and other support services have followed. Organizations, public or private, are told to concentrate on their core services.

Contracting is not just taking place at the fringes of government, but touching almost every aspect of government. Contracting takes place between different levels of government. A government department can sign a performance contract with a government agency. The British Next Steps agencies (James 1995) have been copied throughout the world (Greve 2000). These are special purpose organizations in the U.K. central government that have a framework agreement where specific performance targets are set. Contracting takes places between different sectors. Departments and agencies can also make contracts within themselves so that sub-units or offices are governed by contracts. Governments contract with private for-profit providers and nonprofit providers for the delivery of public services. Contracting takes places between governments and citizens, a trend currently sweeping through the public sectors in Scandinavia. Local governments sign contracts with citizens in order for them to receive welfare benefits. Contracting takes place in various policy areas. Traditionally, contracting has been used for "technical" services like snow removal, building and construction work, cleaning, and road maintenance. In recent years, the trend has been to contract for human services as well (DeHoog 1984; Johnson & Waltzer, eds. 2000; Romzek and Johnston 2002).

CONTRACTING AS A BREAK WITH HIERARCHY? DEFINING CONTRACTUAL GOVERNANCE

Contracting is seen by many as a break with a hierarchical mode of governance and a trend toward an interorganizational network mode of governance (Milward and Provan 1993, 2000). Contracting creates new types of relationships between organizations in the public sector and in the private sector. In order to function in this new relationship, governments must learn how to be "smart buyers" that can enable and manage an array of providers in networks (Kettl 1993). When governments contract extensively with private for-profit and/or nonprofit providers, the government risks being "hollowed out" (Milward and Provan 1993), but it also has the opportunity to become an "enabling" government (Walsh 1995). Contracting raises new demands for public managers, as they must manage contracts and providers in addition to managing and motivating their own staff and mastering their own resources. The result is a mode of governance that differs from the traditional governmental model associated with Wilson and Weber's focus on hierarchy and order. In this book, we use the term "contractual governance" to cover the mode of governance that occurs when the public provider buys services and products from providers through a contractual agreement. As we shall see later, contractual governance implies three steps for governments (Kettl 1993). First, the governments must find out "what to buy." This involves the creation of performance targets and indicators. Next, the governments must find out "whom to buy from." This means that the governments must scan the market to find suitable providers. If there are no available providers, the governments must consider if they have the capacity to create new markets. Third, the governments must find out "what has been bought." This involves monitoring, evaluating, and controlling to see that the output is consistent with the performance measures set out in the contract.

GLOBAL CONTRACTING

Contracting is not a mode of governance that is confined to a few countries. As part of the wider privatization movement, contracting has been taking place on a global scale (Hodge 2000). In this section, we briefly consider the main experiences. In the United States, contracting has been known for a long time. As Kettl (1993) remarked, almost all types of services have been contracted out somewhere in the world. Contracting picked up in the United States in the early 1970s. E. S. Savas (2000), an early proponent, claims almost to have originated the practice with his proposal to contract out snow plowing in New York City. According to Savas, the term "privatization" was coined by management guru Peter Drucker in the 1960s. In the United States, contracting takes place in the federal government through the implementation of circular A-76. President George W. Bush has put contracting on the top of his management agenda, although some contracting schemes have been reconsidered as a result of the 9-11 terror attacks. The Aviation and Transportation Security Act, signed by the president, states that airport security is the responsibility of government employees and cannot be contracted out to private firms. At the local level, contracting has been a trend throughout the 1990s in U.S. local governments, where more and more services were contracted out to private companies and nonprofit organizations (Martin ICMA 1999; Johnson and Waltzer 2000). Contracting is also a long-time feature in Britain, where former prime minister Margaret Thatcher initiated the policy in the 1980s. Britain introduced its compulsory competitive tendering scheme under the Thatcher government. When the Blair government came to power, the compulsory competitive tendering was superseded by a new scheme called "Best Value" (Vincent-Jones 1999). Contracting out through competitive tendering was no longer compulsory, but local governments were encouraged to put their services out to a public tender. The Best Value scheme gave local governments tools to pursue the policy actively. The latest information from Britain shows that Best Value has not lived up to its intentions, and the Blair government is considering how to reintroduce a tougher stance to induce local governments to increase contracting out.

Perhaps the most widely quoted examples are from Australia and New Zealand, where contracting out has been a feature of the New Public Management movement since the 1980s (Domberger and Hall 1996). By now, both countries have a rich experience of contracting for public services. Although their various governments have pushed contracting relentlessly, the evidence is still mixed at best (Boston 1999). Contracting has put performance measurement on the map and helped governments get their priorities in order, but it has not solved all their problems. There are still problems with finding professional providers in certain policy areas, and there are still problems in getting agents to do what their principals tell them. In Europe, contracting has been a dominant feature in many governments and local governments (Wegener 1998; Bryntse 2000; Almquist 2001). Contracting is used both as contracting out and as performance contracting in Europe, as we shall see later.

DOES CONTRACTING INFLUENCE PERFORMANCE?

A long-standing debate in the literature on contracting is whether contracting influences performance. While we do not want to explore that question in this book, a brief comment on the debate may put the discussions in this book into proper context. One of the chief aims of contracting out is to influence performance and to get a better output. Perhaps the most-cited reason for contracting public services is to reduce costs and to spare the taxpayers money. Proponents of contracting out have consistently argued that contracting out produces savings of around 20 percent. Leading privatization author E. S. Savas (2000) quotes the 20 percent in his seminal work on privatization. Domberger (1998) refers to an early study he conducted in the 1980s of garbage collection in the United Kingdom. In this study, Domberger and his colleague found savings of around 20 percent. Other studies have been more skeptical. Boyne (1998) has examined service improvement and cost savings in local governments in the United States. He found little evidence for the 20 percent savings claim and calls the evidence sketchy at best.

Australian professor Graeme Hodge (2000) has made the most thorough study of contracting out. Hodge has conducted a meta-analysis of all empirical studies in the English language of contracting out. Hodge finds that the "20%" rule of thumb so often mentioned in contracting out discussions comes from the aforementioned study by Domberger and colleague in the 1980s. That figure has been propelled into folk wisdom, without much critical examination. Hodge's own studies show a more sophisticated result. He finds that cost savings are connected to contracting out, but they are less than the acclaimed 20 percent. If you look for an average figure, it lies between 7 percent and 12 percent, but an average figure is difficult to obtain because studies vary a great deal from policy area to policy area. Most savings are connected to cleaning and garbage collection, which is also where most of the studies have been conducted. Another well-examined policy area is education. U.S. and U.K. studies are overrepresented in Hodge's material, whose data dates back to the 1980s and ends in the mid-1990s. Hodge not only measures the financial results of contracting out but also looks at its social and political impacts. He finds that a greater portion of women than men have been made redundant by contracting out policy decisions.

The empirical studies by Boyne and Hodge are among the most reliable, and they bring a healthy dose of scientific evidence to counter the exaggerated claims that some privatization proponents tend to make from time to time. The studies also tell us that we must be careful when assessing contracting out policies. Many factors may influence the results, including constitutional, political, economic, organizational, and social factors.

ARE THERE LIMITS TO THE NEW CONTRACTUALISM?

In a review of the New Zealand experience, Professor Anne Yeatman (1995) spoke about "the New Contractualism," indicating that contracting for public services is more than a governance mode; it also introduces a new language into the public sector. The traditional public sector has been characterized by hierarchy, loyalty to the state, impartiality, and equal rights for citizens. The new contractualism redefines much of the language and many of the practices of the public sector. A client is no longer a client, but a customer (Fountain 2001). A government minister who might wish to direct policy in a certain way also has to consider the contractual obligations that already exist. Likewise, citizens may find that the way services are provided to them has been settled in contractual terms. The advent of the new contractualism prompts the question of whether there are limits to the policy areas in which contractual governance can be applied. The answer is by no means straightforward. Prison contracting is thought by many to push the limits of what can be contractualized, yet there are private prisons in the United States, the United Kingdom, and Australia. In Denmark, the possibility of prisons run by private companies was mentioned by the government in relation to public-private partnerships. As Kettl (1993) notes, almost all kinds of public services and tasks have been contracted out somewhere at some point. Human services are currently being put on contract in many places in the United States and in the rest of the world as well. While there are plenty of stories about how contracting does not work, there are equally many stories about how contracting can provide better service, sometimes at lower costs. Proponents of contracting, like E. S. Savas (2000), see a huge potential in government contracting, while others remain more skeptical. Domberger (1998, 205), however, makes the point that there is a long way to go before all the possibilities for government contracting have been explored. If there are limits, they have not been reached yet. The only thing that is certain is that the limits are being pushed all the time by various governments as well as by current and potential providers in search of new markets.

THE CONTINUOUS PRESENCE OF CONTRACTING ON THE POLICY AGENDA

Despite having debated contracting out for more than twenty-five years, there are few signs that governments keep on marketing the policy toward voters and subnational governments. From one point of view, the continuous presence of contracting out on governments' policy agenda is not surprising. The limits of contracting have not yet been reached in earnest, and although there are stories that can damage contracting out, other areas and newly elected governments around the world are willing to include it in their political platforms (Denmark being a recent example). From another point of view, the presence of contracting out is a riddle. If empirical studies continue to show that the real impact of contracting out is not as great as expected and that the governments do not save nearly so much money as promised, then why should contracting be attractive to the governments? Like a rubber duck in a bathtub, the contracting out question continues to pop up and refuses to be drowned or forgotten.

In this book, we examine how governments will not allow the question of contracting out to go away. Our examination draws on inspiration of the advocacy coalition framework developed by Sabatier and Jenkins-Smith (1993, 1999). In this framework, coalitions debate and battle over policies while producing and drawing upon a base of "technical knowledge" of the subject in question. Providing "evidence" valid enough to be taken seriously by decision makers can encourage various coalitions to continue to influence the policy process. The advocacy coalition framework opens up the possibility that at some point the coalitions might agree on a mutual policy because the evidence has proved strong enough from a professional point of view. This is in contrast to most interest group theories that assume that resources and political strategies will pave the way for "victory" for one side of the battle.

THE NEED FOR GETTING THE CONTRACTING PROCESS RIGHT

Why do governments want to contract out services, and what are the main hindrances they encounter? According to specialist Simon Domberger (1998, 51), the benefits of contracting are specialization (the government concentrates on specifying and controlling performance measures), market discipline (transactions take place under contracts), flexibility (the governments can use a wide range of public and private providers), and cost savings (the governments can purchase services at the same level of quality, but at a lower price—this point is debatable and discussed in the literature). In Domberger's assessment, the costs of contracting are "hollowed out governments," loss of skills, loss of corporate memory, weakened innovative capacity, and transition costs (when employees are fired, but may have to be employed again if the government regains the service production responsibility in the future). How can costs and benefits be compared to decide whether contracting is a good idea or not?

To let the benefits outweigh the costs, the contractual governance process must be examined. According to Domberger (1998, 71), the question is "whether contracts can be designed and implemented so that the benefits exceed the costs." For Domberger, the answer is positive, because the contracting process can be constructed to avoid, or at least minimize, costs. For others, like Hodge (2000), there is less certainty as to whether the costs can be minimized. As Domberger writes (1998, 71) "For successful contracting to occur organizations need to identify the market conditions which generate potential benefits, and they must be able to appropriate

them at a reasonable cost. Their contractual arrangements need to combine control with flexibility."

From this point of view, whether contracting works out or not is dependent on how well the contract is written and how well the contractual governance process is planned. Contracting is then not inherently "good" or
"bad," but a tool and a process that can be managed and governed—in
short, the process can be influenced by political and other actors.

A number of studies have looked into how the contractual governance
process is structured (Wallin 1997; Brown and Potoski 2003). They identify
several variables, among which are the following: Policy design must be
well prepared; politicians and top management must back the process
fully; employees must be consulted before major restructurings; there
must be enough competition in the marketplace; the performances of the
providers must be easy to measure and evaluate; citizens, as customers,
must be able to state their preferences clearly.

The big question is whether the contractual governance process can be
nurtured and polished so that smooth contractual governance will occur.
Kettl (1993) argues that there will be inherent challenges in a public marketplace, one reason being that full or perfect competition is not likely for
many public services.

THE PROFILE OF THE CONTRACT STATE

Christopher Pollitt (2001) has characterized the profile of the new public management version of the public sector as a lean state that contracts
for public services through a variety of external providers from the for-
profit and nonprofit private sector. Similar profiles can be found in the
works of Milward and Provan (2000), Kettl (1993), Domberger (1998), and
Savas (2000). Responsible politicians will act more as "purchasers" of
services, and to aid them in this respect a new breed of contract specialists
and managers needs to be trained. Many of the profiles of the imagined
contract state resemble the features of the "competition model" described
by DeHoog (1990). However, what many of the authors mentioned here
also note is how difficult it is to get from the present state of affairs to the
contract state. The likely result is to end somewhere in-between, which
raises new issues for the management and governance of public purchasing organizations.

THE PURPOSE AND QUESTIONS OF THIS BOOK

The purpose of this book is to examine the contractual governance
process and to determine which factors influence it. The contractual governance process is our dependent variable. Already, as we have seen, con-

siderable evidence exists concerning the contractual governance process. Most studies on contractual governance examine only one institutional setting. Romzek and Johnston's (2002) influential studies discuss contracting in local governments in Kansas. Milward and Provan's (2000) well-known studies on contracting in interorganizational networks study contracts in Arizona. Thereby, the institutional variable is held constant as other variables (political pressure, transaction costs, number of providers on the market) are explored as independent variables.

The book is written from a public management perspective in political science and public administration. Contracting has been studied in other disciplines, most notably the new economics of organizations (Moe 1984; Williamson 1975, 1985, 1996), from a sociolegal perspective (Campbell and Vincent Jones, eds., 1996), and of course in public and private law. Our perspective is public management, and we are especially interested in what we here refer to as "contractual governance," the contract implementation and management process that takes place when contracting for public services.

What is missing in the public management literature is a genuinely comparative assessment of the contractual governance process. In other words, what is the impact of the institutional setting on the contractual governance process? A number of studies draw on examples from around the world, but only a select few employ a comparative framework. Hodge (2000) studies empirical studies on contracting out and samples evidence (reported in English) from around the world. His studies assess the impact of contracting out, but his meta-analysis does not allow him to discuss the institutional setting at length. Savas (2000) draws on examples from around the world in his seminal study on contracting out, but he does not examine the cases in a systematic way. Christensen and Lægreid's edited volume on New Public Management (2001) is a comparative study on public management in Sweden, Norway, Australia, and New Zealand, but the authors pay only limited attention to contracting out and give more attention to privatization as sale of assets. Bryntse (2000) studied contracting out in local governments in Sweden, Germany, and Britain and came up with empirical results concerning the contracting process. Wegener (2000) is perhaps the study closest to this book. Wegener has compared contracting out in the United States and Germany. His findings are important but, unfortunately for non-Germans, only reported in the German language.

A point long established in the literature on the new institutionalism is that "institutions matter" (Scott 1995). In the present study, we take this thesis as our point of departure, as we want to examine how contractual institutions influence the contractual governance process. To do this, we compare the experience of contracting for public services in local governments in the United States with contracting for public services in local governments in Scandinavia. Before we explain our reasons for comparing the United States and Scandinavia, let us elaborate on the institutional argument.

Institutions can be understood as regulative, normative, and cognitive structures that shape and guide human action (Scott 1995). For local governments that contract for public services, this means to care for contract regulations, the norms and values that guide public service provision, and the interpretations and cognitive maps the actors have of contracts in the public sector and the private sector. For example, a Scandinavian local government cannot contract out a public service task worth more than a certain level of euros without taking into account the European Union rules for contracting out. The structure of a European Union tender is of tremendous importance to how a government thinks about performance measures and how contracting out is actually implemented. Another example would be a rural local government that might consider contracting out care for its elderly. The rural area may have a long tradition of not engaging private for-profit companies in the delivery of public services. Therefore, contracting out to a nationwide (or even global) company will break the norms and values of that community. Although the government may be ideologically committed to contracting out, the norms and values of the community may oppose a decision to contract out. A third example would be a local government in the United States whose public sector is heavily unionized. The cognitive mind-set of employees is likely to be disposed against contracting out, and therefore the contracting process will suffer blows along the way.

In this book, we prefer to use the term "the contract culture" to describe the regulative, normative, and cognitive structures that guide the actions of local governments in contractual governance. The contract culture has turned out to be important in studies of individual nations, as Cooper (2003) so convincingly has demonstrated for the United States. By going into a nation's historical experience with contracting out, we can examine how the regulative, normative, and cognitive structures influence how contracting out is implemented in today's societies.

Why compare the United States and Scandinavia? While there are many studies on contracting out in the United States, there is not a great deal of "policy transfer" or "knowledge transfer" to Europe and Scandinavia. Many Europeans assume that local governments in the United States have privatized almost everything and that the public sector is small and lean. Of course, this is not so. Many U.S. local governments face the same challenges as everybody else, and public workers are proud of their jobs and of their local government. For a European, the extraordinary factor to discover is that contracting out is precisely as controversial in a U.S. local government as in a European local government if it has not been introduced before. Therefore, it is useful to adapt and compare experiences from the United States with other parts of the world. Experience with contracting is a global phenomenon, and it will be interesting to know whether institutions will influence contractual governance and how. The choice of Scandinavia is partly pragmatic and partly due to our research strategy. Pragmatic, because we are Scandinavians (Danes) and know the public sector in Sweden, Norway, and Denmark well. And partly academic, because we think that the study of contracting can benefit from more comparative studies that can shed light on the supposed "uniqueness" of each contractual governance process.

The research questions we examine in this book can be summarized as follows:

1. Why does contracting continue to be on the policy agenda?
2. Which factors determine the success of the contractual governance process so that benefits outweigh costs?
3. How does a country's "contract culture" influence the contractual governance process?

Our working hypotheses are as follows: Contracting is a battle between two or more political coalitions that provide knowledge on contracting out. The factors that determine the contracting agenda are the political context surrounding contracting out, establishment of a combined and dynamic smart buyer function, the number and status of private providers, and the evaluation and accountability structure that governments establish to keep track of performance measures.

METHODOLOGY

The research in this study employs a plurality of methods. First, we conduct a literature review to find out what other studies on contractual governance have shown. We have searched the literature on contracting through databases of monographs, edited volumes, and journal articles. We have paid special attention to what are considered leading journals on contractual governance: *Public Administration Review*, the *Journal of Public Administration Research and Theory*, *Public Administration*, *Public Management Review*, and *Administration and Society*. This literature review has helped us to establish a theoretical model on contractual governance, which is used later in the book.

Second, we adopt a comparative framework to study contractual governance. Comparative studies are well rehearsed in the literature on public management reform (Pollitt and Bouckaert 2000; Christensen and Lægreid 2001), but not used enough in studies on contracting more specifically (see, however, Bryntse 2000 and Wegener 2000). In our comparative framework, we draw on insights from the established scholarly work on the comparative method in political studies (Peters 1998).

Third, we have made use of policy analysis to discuss why and how contractual governance has remained at the policy agenda. We have taken our point of departure in the advocacy coalition framework (ACF) developed by Sabatier and Jenkins-Smith (1993, 1998, 1999), which is considered one of the key new theories of the policy process (Sabatier, ed., 1999). One of the key advantages of the ACF is that it allows the researcher to look at coalitions for and against contracting out from a wider angle than the usual interest group studies. An advocacy coalition advancing contracting out can include politicians, public managers, interest groups, and firms as well as journalists and researchers. The ACF examines how deep core beliefs and secondary beliefs can be changed, and they point to the role of mediators to combine belief systems. Thereby, the ACF postulates that policy learning is possible and that expert knowledge can form the basis for mutual understanding. While some have criticized this for being too "instrumental," the ACF offers a fruitful theory to examine why contracting out is still high on the public management policy agenda despite now having made private companies an integral part of all public service delivery systems.

Fourth, we have conducted two in-depth case studies in Scandinavia and the United States. The cases are the local government of Odense in Denmark, and Dane County, Wisconsin. Research on the cases was done in 2002. Before presenting the case studies, we analyze the available evidence on contracting experience in human services in the United States and Scandinavia.

Fifth, we have conducted a survey of performance contracting within the public sector, that is, where one public sector organization contracts with other lower-tier public organizations for specific outputs and outcomes. The survey looks at contractual governance in the Danish municipalities. The survey was mailed to all 275 municipalities, and 158 municipalities answered. The survey results are presented and discussed here and related to studies of performance contracting in the United States.

THE STRUCTURE OF THE BOOK

This first chapter introduces the concept of a contract and contractual governance, and presents our research questions.

In chapter 2, "Theories of Contracts," we examine hard and soft versions of contracts and combine them with behavioral assumptions of the logic of consequentiality and the logic of appropriateness. The result is a table describing the conditions necessary for modern contractual governance to function. Next, we examine more specific studies of the contract implementation and management process. The chapter ends with an assessment of theoretical model building in the literature up to now.

In chapter 3, "Contractual Governance," we present and discuss our theoretical model for discussing contractual governance and the contract implementation and management process. The model builds from the original contents of the "Kettl-model" and incorporates insights from other researchers like Romzek and Johnston, while also including the concept of "the contract culture" to emphasize the importance of the institutional environment of contracting.

In chapter 4, "Policy Change and Learning in Contracting Out," we present and use the advocacy coalition framework (ACF) of Sabatier and Jenkins-Smith to analyze the development of the contracting out agenda in Denmark. Using an empirical study on agenda data from 1995 to 2000, we examine the strategies and composition of two competition advocacy coalitions in contracting out.

In chapter 5, "Contractual Governance in the United States and Scandinavia," we examine the available evidence on the contracting process in Scandinavia and the United States during the last 10 years. Using a comparative perspective, we try to assess the influence of different variables on contracting experiences in those two parts of the world.

In chapter 6, "Case Studies of Contractual Governance," we present empirical data from two in-depth case studies of two local governments: the Odense municipality in Denmark, and Dane County in Wisconsin.

In chapter 7, "Performance-Based Contracting in Local Government," we use empirical data from a nationwide survey conducted in Danish municipalities to analyze contract implementation and management within the public sector, and we contrast the findings with evidence from similar U.S. studies.

In chapter 8, we analyze what happens when contractual governance fails, through a case study of Farum local government.

In chapter 9, "Conclusion: Contractual Governance in a Cross-Cultural Perspective," we present the main findings of our analysis and reexamine the contractual governance model in light of our discussion. We also point to new research areas within the public management study of contractual governance.

2

Theories of Contracts

INTRODUCTION

What is a contract? How is a contract defined? What are the formal and informal features of a contract? What kinds of behavioral assumptions exist for analyzing attitudes and actions in contracting? These questions, which are considered in this chapter, lead up to a focus on contractual governance, a concept that will be explored further in chapter 3.

THE ESSENTIAL FEATURES OF A CONTRACT

A contract can be defined as "agreements concluded on an equal footing by two or more parties who freely consent and who freely settle the terms of their agreement" (Keith, quoted in Martin 1995, 38). A contract will have the following features (Gomard 1996; Martin 1995, 39).

1. It is usually a written agreement between two or more parties.
2. Contracts create rights and duties for the parties only.
3. Sanctions will be enforced if contractual obligations are not met.

Contracts can be understood in "black letter law." The contracts are written documents. They can be a standard document that can be adapted to individual providers. Both parties are bound by the commitment of their signature on the contract. If either party violates the terms, clear sanctions are usually connected to the breach. Bonuses may be connected to the contract in the case of overachievement of the objectives.

When contracting is used as a mode of governance, one party—the principal—buys or demands a service or a product from another party— the agent. This creates a principal-agent relationship. In agency theory, it is assumed that both the principal and the agent are utility maximizers. The problem is that of moral hazard and adverse selection, also called "hidden action" and "hidden information." The principal cannot readily observe the actions of the agent. The principal cannot always have access to information the agent has. Therefore, the principal must design the contract so that actions and information will be unveiled.

If principals are explicit about what they want to achieve and if agents are assigned the task of achieving the stated purpose, then the contract can become subject to clear and unambiguous accountability. This is part of the rationalization of contracts, which again is part of a wider intellectual movement in political and social science: rational choice (Yeatman 1995).

THE EXPANDED FEATURES OF A CONTRACT

In the eyes of many observers, it is not enough to understand the essential features of a contract. People must also grapple with the context of the contracts. The sociologist Emile Durkheim once said that "not everything in a contract is contractual." He meant that the institutions must guarantee that a contract will be taken seriously in any analysis. The political system and the court system must work properly if contract violations are to be sanctioned. Yet it is not necessary or possible to write down every detail in every contract. Furthermore, the contract depends on the parties' attitudes toward the contract. Contracts are entered into in an institutionalized environment. They cannot be understood only in a narrow or "essential" way.

The expanded features of a contract imply what New Zealand professor Anne Yeatman (1995, 124–125) calls "the new contractualism." This involves "a contractualist language making explicit the reciprocal expectations between the parties concerned. Such explicitness is reached through a mixed process of contract and negotiation, often of course in the context of established policies, guidelines or procedures."

Contracts have to rely on some sort of trust-based relationships, according to sociolegal scholars Campbell and Vincent-Jones (1996). Cooperation, however, does not always have to be based on trust, but on the inevitability of cooperation between two or more parties to a contract.

The difficulty with most modern-day policies is that the principals cannot always specify in advance what they want to achieve. Contracts have to be open-ended and to rely on some sort of process control (Williamson 1985).

The expanded features of a contract can be summarized as follows:

1. Contracts are written agreements between two or more parties that take place in a context (political, juridical, economic, and social).
2. Contracts create rights and duties, but not every output measure can be fixed ex-ante, leaving contracts open-ended.
3. Sanctions will be enforced if the contractual obligations are not met, but the trust-based relationship and the need for future co-operation will ensure that sanctions are really the last resort.

HARD AND SOFT VERSIONS OF CONTRACTS

This section introduces the notion of "hard" and "soft" contracts. Building on the preceding discussion, we argue that there are two versions of a contract in the modern-day public sector: the hard contract and the soft contract. The division is well known in the literature on contracting (DeHoog 1990; Domberger 1998, 131).

In the hard version of a contract, the principals (politicians, for example) know what they want to achieve. They specify performance measures. Performance measures are targets that should be met and met accurately. Literature dealing with performance measures and the problems of setting targets goes back to Selznick (1957/1984). The contracts are written documents, which specify in every detail the kind of targets set. The public management task is here to hire contract lawyers to draw up correctly all the details and special features. To engage the providers to deliver the service, a competitive market is the preferred tool. Politics is taken out of the game once the performance measures have been set. If these measures are not met, clear legal standards spell out what will incur and enforce sanctions. The time span is usually short term. Contracts are rebid in a new round of tender.

Williamson (1985) refers to this model as classical (or neoclassical) contracting. This is what DeHoog (1990, 321–324) refers to as "the competition model," which is said to be the "the contracting ideal" in the contracting theory. As DeHoog writes, "In the competition model of contracting out, the government has its choice among several bids and therefore can select the firm that will provide the specified services at the lowest costs" (321).

In the soft version of a contract, principals (politicians, for example) do not know exactly what they want, or they have trouble looking into the future to take account of all possible contingencies. Williamson's (1985) argument is that it is difficult to write a complete contract. Contracts cannot specify all contingencies and aims in every detail. The contract has to leave room for future changes and be flexible enough to provide for organizational and human learning. As DeHoog (1990, 326) comments: "The desired services are not specified in very much detail, although certain elements that officials have made a priority are included." Once a relationship is built, the principal and the agent may have little incentive to break up the relationship. A provider that has done well in a contract period will stand a good chance of having the contract renewed. Although this will be at the expense of other competitors, there are advantages from the point of view of the established provider and the purchaser. The provider can renew and improve the product or the service in stable conditions. The purchaser knows what the provider stands for, and the purchaser does not have to go through costly tender processes. The type of staff needed here is process consultants, who could be trained as contract management specialists from business schools or universities. They do not have to be lawyers.

Sanctions will seldom be used explicitly, because there will be few clear-cut measures to judge by. The performance measures are established and may change during the contract period. The output may be different from the one that the principal originally imagined, but that does not matter if the principal is happy with the current output. In this soft version of a contract, politics is not taken out of the contracting process but is potentially present at all times during the contract period. Politicians can for one reason or another decide to open up old issues. Providers can complain that the politicians' objectives are not easily achievable. All this will be negotiated and dealt with along the way. The provider is never left completely alone in this model, as dialogue is ongoing between the parties to the contract, and only rarely will the courts be involved in dispute settlement. Williamson (1975) referred to the "small numbers problem" when he pointed out that if only a few companies can negotiate with the public purchaser, policy options will be limited for the purchaser.

Williamson (1985) calls this mode of contracting "relational contracting," as opposed to the classical and neoclassical model. DeHoog (1990, 325–329) refers to it as "the negotiation model." In this model, the contract is formed as a closed negotiation between the purchaser and providers that are well known to the purchaser: "The process of negotiation begins with an announcement of the availability of the contracts, but often without a full-scale search or solicitation for all possible contractors. The suppliers who are contacted are limited to previous contractors and possibly, to firms that have expressed an interest in obtaining a contract" (DeHoog 1990, 326). In contrast to the competition model, the relational contract or the negotiation model will make sure that both parties have their objectives fulfilled. In DeHoog's (1990, 327) words, "The parties may see their goals and interests very differently, but they both can achieve certain advantages by a process that adheres to the basic ground rules of fairness, truthfulness and reason as they seek a contract beneficial to both." The negotiation model may be based on a lack of alternatives for each side of the bargaining table. A private provider may see government as its strongest customer and therefore not be willing to skip contractual negotiations because of small upheavals. Many private providers will have a stronger interest in retaining the contract than attaining specific objectives in the contracting process. What the negotiation model promises, according to both Williamson (1985) and DeHoog (1990, 328), is that transaction costs will be reduced in the form of "administrative expertise, staff time, information requirements, advertising, and solicitation costs." Transaction costs can increase, however, if negotiations about performance measurements are repeated too often. This is due to a focus on procedures rather than on specific output. DeHoog (1990, 326) notes how the contract will still leave the government as a "purchaser" with the upper hand in the negotiations. If the negotiations become too intimate, the responsible politicians and the contractors may pursue their private ends (DeHoog 1990, 326).

DeHoog (1990, 329–335) also refers to a third model, "the cooperation model." In this model, there is only one contractor, and the purchaser has no alternatives to choose from. Building on Williamson's (1975) analysis, cooperation is a necessity when there is uncertainty and complexity "about future events, funding, technology, or successful service methods" (DeHoog 1990, 329). DeHoog finds that the cooperation model is especially likely when there are "high capital investment or market entry costs" and the need to enter a long-term commitment to guard the investment. As a government may find it hard to produce the service itself, it has to rely on a private partner, and that partner will want to be assured that the contract is safe for a foreseeable future. In recent years, the cooperation model has been known in the academic and practical literature as public-private partnerships (Linder 1999). While this model is relevant to the wider discussion of public-private cooperation, the specific issue of public-private partnerships will not be dealt with in greater detail here.

Comparing the competition model with the negotiation model (and the cooperative model), DeHoog (1990, 336) notes that, "while the design of the competitive bidding system emphasizes an optimization strategy in seeking and choosing among suppliers, the negotiation and the co-operation designs are more oriented toward an incremental approach in the Simon (1976) tradition." The soft contract is more based on "face-to-face" negotiations and ongoing relationships, while the competition model "relies on the formal process of soliciting, awarding, and administering contracts."

TABLE 2.1
Hard and Soft Contracts

	Hard / classical and neoclassical	Soft / relational
Purpose	To secure a specific objective	To secure a specific value
Contract document	Detailed and often lengthy	General and short, spells out broad aims
Time frame	Short term	Long term
Relationship	Adversary	Mutuality
Control	Strict control of clear performance indicators	Broad control based on dialogue regarding attainment of mutual aims
Sanctions	Sanctions specified and clear	Sanctions unclear and more normative than to do with strict regulations
Workforce at HQ	Performance setters and contract lawyers	Policy and management specialists
Role of politics	Politics is taken out of the process once the contract is signed	Politics continues to be a part of the contracting process
Risk	Risk shifting from principal to agent	Risk sharing between parties

Source: Based on DeHoog 1990; Domberger 1998, table 7.3, 131; Greve 2000.

BEHAVIORAL ASSUMPTIONS IN CONTRACTING

In the literature on contracting, the behavioral assumptions are often implicit. Nearly all researchers would confirm that actors act under some kind of information constraint and that they are only "limited rational" in Simon's sense (1945). However, it might further our understanding of contracts and the contracting process to get a clearer picture of the behavioral aspect of the people involved in contracting. Williamson, a researcher whose behavioral assumptions are clear, is a part of "the new economics of organization" school in economics and organizational science (Moe 1984). For Williamson, actors act in opportunistic ways, where opportunism is defined as "self-interest with guile" (Williamson 1985, 47). Others, for example Domberger (1998), do not state their specific behavioral assumptions.

Behavioral assumptions may have an impact on the way a contracting process is likely to function. If a government has drawn up what it thinks is a classical contract, but the agent acts as if it is a partnership venture, then the contract might lose its significance as a governance and management tool. Williamson assumes that actors will try to get the most out of the contract. But he also knows that it is not possible to write a contract that will fully cover all contingencies in the future. Therefore, Williamson discusses the relational contract, which allows flexibility in the contracting period, but still takes the actor's original strategy and basic goals into account.

The literature on behavior by political actors is huge. Here, we take our departure from March and Olsen's (1989) famous division between the "logic of consequentiality" and the "logic of appropriateness," which is inspired by institutional analysis. In the logic of consequentiality, actors follow a rational strategy for attaining specific goals. Actors have ordered preferences and are able to choose from two or more alternatives. The preferences of actors are fixed. Events during a process will not alter the original goals set by an actor. In the logic of appropriateness, actors do what is expected of them by fellow actors and their superiors or by the normative and cognitive schemes present in society and in organizations. When a newcomer to an organization goes to his or her first day at work, that person will try to get a feeling for the atmosphere of the organization and to figure out the prevailing ideas and norms. If the norm is to take lunch at 12 o'clock and to consume the lunch with all colleagues together, then the person will follow suit, gradually adopting the norms of the organization as his or her own.

If we combine the behavioral assumptions with the notion of hard and soft contracts mentioned previously, we get an interesting table, which we can use to discuss the conditions for contractual governance. (See Table 2.2.)

In box 1, we find the most common way of framing discussions on contracting. Both parties to the contract bring their own interests and objectives to the bargaining table. Each one will insist that goals are specified and detailed and that sanctions are spelled out and clear. The hard contract will take care of the logic of consequentiality and encompasses rational actors' strategies. In the principal-agent framework, both have something to bring to the table as well, although the relationship takes place in governance mode. The principal has a job to be carried out and the resources and sanctions to apply to the agent. The agent has the information needed to do the job, but may apply it tactically and strategically. As the real action of the agent cannot be controlled fully, the principal must influence the agent to comply with the principal's aims.

In box 2, the story is different. Either both parties or just one will strive to achieve mutual aims between the parties, or wider societal aims deemed worthy by a larger group (or a larger cause). In this case, a

TABLE 2.2
Behavioral Assumptions in Contracting

	Hard contract	Soft contract
Logic of consequentiality	1	3
Logic of appropriateness	2	4

detailed and specific contract may not be useful. But a hard contract can limit the interest of the actors in the long term. It can also lead to unnecessary transaction costs, if one party tries to control the information and actions of the other party by detailed means, even though that information and actions could be have been detected through simple dialogue between the two parties.

In box 3, a soft contract is supposed to regulate actors that both follow the logic of consequentiality. This can lead to abuse by both parties, as no adequate measures in the contract regulate narrow interest-seeking behavior. Of course, it could be in the rational interest of both parties to agree on mutual aims (witness the prisoner's dilemma in game theory), but that will not always be the case in real life. The soft contract might here be a document that both parties to the contract need not take into account in their real-life strategies, which could make it irrelevant, as it may regulate nothing in the end.

Box 4 combines a soft contract and the logic of appropriateness. Both parties enter the contract with the best intentions and aim to find mutual solutions to problems. Objectives are not spelled out in detail, and the flexibility along the way is appreciated by both parties to the contract.

CONTRACTUAL GOVERNANCE

To govern and manage by contract, it is essential to know what type of contract regulates the relationship and what kind of strategy actors are pursuing when entering a contract. Contractual governance is about guiding between hard and soft contracts and between different logics of action. Several authors (see Bryntse 2000 and DeHoog 1990) have pointed out that the hard and the soft contracts need to be alternatives. A real-life contract can contain both "hard" and "soft" elements. One way is to have the "hard" contract as a basis and then build "soft" measures into the contract step-by-step. With the different logics of action we find a similar story. In some instances, actors may follow the logic of consequentiality, and they need to be faced with that in negotiations. In other instances, actors may follow the logic of appropriateness. There is not necessarily only one best way to conduct a contractual relationship. For academic analysis, the type of contracts and the actors' strategies must be identified. The practioner, the principal, the agent, or simply the partner must take into account what kind of contract they are being regulated by (or will regulate by) and what kind of strategies the other party is intending to follow.

For academic analysis, the study of contractual governance is the study of how governments and organizations are coping with hard and soft contracts and what kind of action logic is guiding their strategy. Governing through a hard contract seems more plausible if preferences of the actors are fixed and objectives are sought in the short term, while governing through a soft contract is more plausible with actors following the logic of appropriateness in a more incremental way (see also DeHoog 1990). The difficulties in terms of governing clearly lie in the two "odd" boxes, box 2 (hard contract and logic of appropriateness) and box 4 (soft contract and logic of consequentiality), although, as we have seen, Williamson's model of relational, soft contracting does assume that actors follow the logic of consequentiality. It does seem as if the soft model will be more flexible in adapting to changes in the environments of the organizations (DeHoog 1990, 337).

AN INSTITUTIONALIST PERSPECTIVE ON THE CONTRACT CULTURE

In Durkheim's words, to repeat, "not everything in a contract is contractual." Both hard and soft contracts rest on institutions already established in society. Thus, a contract negotiation depends on a juridical system and the establishment of prisons if sanctions are not met and one party is convicted of fraud. The study of contracts must therefore also examine the formal and informal rules that govern the narrower contracting relationship. In this book, we term these formal and informal rules "the contract culture." As in institutional analysis, the contract culture is not static, but should be seen in a developmental perspective. The contract culture will change in different societies. Some rules will be steadfast, but others may be altered, both by action and by environmental pressure.

STUDIES OF CONTRACTUAL GOVERNANCE IN THE PUBLIC SECTOR

The types of contracts (hard and soft) and the behavioral assumptions of contract actors form the basis for understanding the institutional conditions under which contractual governance is studied. It is constructive to look at contractual governance as a contract implementation and management process. In this section, we discuss the main findings of studies that have examined contractual governance understood as the implementation and management process in specific contract cultures.

Kettl (1993) is the now-classic study of contractual governance—and the basis for the model we develop in the next chapter. Kettl examined what he calls "the competition prescription" and then relates that ideal model to the institutional features of the public sector, whereby he demonstrates that management and governance questions are not as straightforward as anticipated in the competition model. Kettl used four case studies as the empirical basis for his analysis on contractual governance. They were as different as the Superfund project on environmental cleanup and the contracting of telecommunication services. In addition, he surveyed the literature and the experience of state and local government contracting in the United States.

Kettl asks three questions, which form the basis of what we call "the Kettl model" in this book: What to buy? Whom to buy from? What has been bought? The first question allows him to examine the reasons politicians give for contracting and the possibilities of putting public tasks in a contract. The second question allows him to examine the type and structure of markets for public services. He finds that markets are seldom competitive as in the economic textbooks. The third question allows him to look at the issue of evaluation and control when local governments try to assess the quality and the quantity of what they have bought.

Kettl offers a balanced view of the contracting process and the possibilities of contracting out. At the beginning of the book, he notes how almost every service has been contracted out at some time somewhere in the world, thereby warning that there is no carved-in-stone principle governing what kind of services can be contracted out. He shows that contracting out is a long-standing phenomenon in government, going back at least to before the establishment of the United States as a federal state (the army led by George Washington had to rely on contractual arrangements for soldiers, weapons, and food). He also notes that the post–World War II history has been full of what he calls public-private partnerships, but what are also referred to as contractual arrangements. In many ways, Kettl's study is termed a classic, a well-deserved term because it deals with many aspects of contractual governance that still occupy governments and public managers around the world. Kettl's discussion of management and governance problems at the end of his book remains full of insights, which we draw upon in this book.

Savas (1987, 2000) offers a rich description of contractual governance processes. Savas was the first one to use the term "privatization" consistently in writing on the matter, and his books on privatization are classics as well. Savas's approach differs somewhat from Kettl's approach. First of all, Savas is normative in his writings, as he makes no secret of his backing of privatization policy. In the foreword to the new edition of his book on privatization, Savas relates to the readers how the privatization ideas that he once championed so vigorously have now become standard policies in many governments around the world. For Savas this is good news; he clearly prefers privatization and private delivery of services to public delivery of services. Savas has conducted empirical studies himself (see, for example, Savas 2002 on welfare service delivery in New York City). Savas uses empirical material as illustrations in his books. He draws on many studies, including his own, but he draws on them highly selectively. His books cannot be said to give balanced views on contracting out. Savas writes about the contracting process in the form of a set of guidelines, wherein he describes the contracting process in 12 steps. For the practitioner, the politician or public manager as policy-maker, Savas's description of the contracting process resembles a strategic and tactical plan that can be followed step-by-step; the end result is a successful implementation of contracting out in a given state. Savas does not seem to take the "contract culture" into account specifically, but it must be assumed that he is well aware of it, as he has consulted with various governments around the world about privatization and contracting out. In almost no case does Savas say he prefers the hierarchical solutions inside the public sector. Savas will always argue, it seems, for the private service delivery option.

Wallin (1997) is a study of a contractual governance process in a single administrative entity in the United States. On the basis of that empirical experience, Wallin raises several issues concerning the proper implementation of contracting out initiatives. One of the key findings is that the "policy rationale" must be quite clear for politicians and public managers before they engage in contracting out.

Domberger (1998) is a well-written and well-researched study of the design and implementation of contractual relationships. As Domberger's book is a textbook on "the contracting organization" (the title of his book), it cannot count as a study of the contractucal governance process as such. But among books on contracting, it is unique in considering examples from the public sector and the private sector on an equal basis. Domberger's key point is that it is how governments (or firms) write the contracts that will determine their success, not so much whether the benefits of contracting outweigh the costs of contracting in a static analysis. Domberger puts contracting in a wider perspective in terms of the evolution and developments of company strategy and business contexts. Domberger is reluctant to say that contracting will go on forever, because of changes in corporations' investment divestiture and downsizing in some instances and mergers in other instances (the latter being an unfavorable condition for contracting). However, Domberger is certain that considering all the experiments going on in the public sector and the private sector, contracting is going to remain on the policy and implementation agenda for a long time to come.

Hodge (2000) has examined the available empirical evidence on contracting out performance. Hodge uses a meta-analytic framework, which enables him to conduct an analysis of all the available studies with statistical significant results. Hodge points to several factors that influence contract implementation and management. Objectives are not always made clear, and often the rationale for pursuing the contracting option is political. Hodge confirms that one of the effects of contracting is cost savings, but he rejects the 20% figure that has been circulating in policy debates since the 1980s. He estimates the figure to be somewhere between 8% and 14% on average (not considering transaction costs) (Hodge 2000, 129).

Most of the savings are shown in U.S. studies in cleaning, refuse collection, and maintenance services. He finds that few studies say anything about the quality of the services, which leaves him to conclude that "as best we know at present, contracting does not reduce or increase quality, as a general rule" (156). While management accountability may have improved, Hodge (156) finds evidence that "openness to scrutiny and accessibility to government information have not."

Bryntse (2000) has studied contracting out in a comparative perspective. Bryntse analyzes four different services in three different countries: Germany, Britain, and Sweden. Using a combination of the new economics of organization, sociological institutional theory, and theories of network governance in industrial studies, Bryntse analyzes how contractual governance works in different institutional settings, what we here call "contract culture."

Wegener (2000) has studied contracting out in local governments in Germany and the United States. The work is only published in the German language.

Johnson and Waltzer (2000) offer evidence from the United States about various aspects of contracting in the public sector, including the contractual governance process. Their findings are mainly in the form of case studies (for example, of Charlotte, N.C.) where they find that a well-prepared policy and attention to the employees' engagement and backup to the process are of importance. Charlotte has seen contracting as a key part of the local government's strategy and not just a tool to be used in selected policy areas. The same experience is usually mentioned in other high-profile cities where contracting forms the basis for the mayor's political strategy (Bertelsen 2000; Goldsmith 1997).

Milward and Provan (2000) have studied contracting in local government for a number of years. Their empirical material comes from a study of a network delivery system in the mental health sector in Arizona. Milward and Provan's studies involved both public and private providers. The authors have concentrated on four cases of in-depth case studies, from which they try to build a theory of, primarily, how networks are governed (Milward and Provan 2000). They show how networks are governed through contractual relationships. One of their key findings is that to be effective, networks of contractual relations require stability. Thereby, Milward and Provan go against the "competition model" of contracting that we wrote about earlier. In some of their writings (Milward and Provan 1998), they have applied principal-agent theory to their empirical material to test new hypotheses.

Romzek and Johnston (2000, 2001, 2002) have studied contracting in Kansas in the United States for a number of years; their studies are some of the most comprehensive ongoing studies around. They use the same method as Milward and Provan, with in-depth case studies of a small number of cases. The empirical study concerns five contracting cases from social services programs related to Medicaid and welfare programs: case management for elderly Medicaid clients, Medicaid managed care for welfare families, employment preparation services statewide for welfare recipients, employment preparation services (comprehensive pilot for one location) for welfare recipients, and foster care adoption services for children legally under state custody because of child abuse or neglect (Romzek and Johnston 2002, appendix 2). Their research method relies on qualitative case studies (following Yin 1989). They conducted 80 interviews during four waves of interviews, from the spring of 1997 to the summer of 2000. Building on their empirical research, Romzek and Johnston (2002) outlined a theoretical model on contract implementation and management effectiveness. Effectiveness is the dependent variable, understood by Romzek and Johnston (2002, 430–431) as "the capacity of the state to design, implement, and manage contracts for social services. This includes the capacity of the state to obtain timely and accurate reporting from the contractor and the ability of the state to use that reported information to evaluate performances and correct deficiencies." They grant that their ratings are "relative" as they use their original case study "as base case" (presumably this case was then exemplary).

Romzek and Johnston (2002) emphasize seven factors that have a positive impact on effectiveness: healthy levels of provider competition, resource adequacy, in-depth planning for contractor performance measurement, intensive training for state contract management staff, evaluation of contractor staff capacity, evaluation of contractor financial management capacity, and the theoretical integrity of the rationale for contracting. They also mention three factors that they hypothesize have a negative impact on contracting implementation and management effectiveness: the political strength of client advocacy groups, the complexity of subcontractor relationships, and risk shifting to the contractor.

The Romzek and Johnston model is one of the most elaborate models to date. In some ways it can be combined with elements of the original Kettl model (as we shall see), and the authors acknowledge Kettl's work in their research. A number of questions can be raised regarding their research. Are cases in Kansas sufficient to build a model of contract implementation and management effectiveness? This critique, however, can be applied to most case studies. Second, in what ways does the contract culture of Kansas have an impact on the contract implementation and management process? We get only a little information on the history of contracting in Kansas compared to other states in the United States, but it must be assumed that the authors possess an in-depth knowledge of this subject. Still, there is enough to build on and be inspired by to make this one of the key studies of contracting.

Cooper (2003) has conducted an analysis of contractual governance in the United States using empirical illustrations from a large number of cases. Cooper follows in the steps of Kettl's process model. The key question at the outset is how politicians and public managers can "get a good deal on behalf of the public." Cooper shows how the contracting process is deeply related to what we have called "the contract culture" in the United States. Especially, Cooper examines how the contract culture in the legal sense contributes to the understanding of contractual governance. Cooper pays special attention to what kind of interest governments and contractors have in terminating their relationship. This could relate to DeHoog's point, when she examined the competition model versus the negotiation and the cooperative models, showing how "soft" contracts make it harder for contractual partners to separate from each other.

Brown and Pototski (2003) have examined contractual governance in the United States with special emphasis on how local governments handle the question of transaction costs. As few studies examine empirical experience with transaction costs, this study is most welcome. Brown and Potoski are able to show how local governments seem to adapt to the prospect of transaction costs. Services that are likely to generate high transaction costs are not contracted out. Services that generate few transaction costs are contracted out. Thereby, local governments are able to handle the issue of transaction costs, and transaction costs are not natural in all contracting out decisions. Their research brings good news to those practioners who want to contract out at the local level and who are confident in the intellectual capacity of local government politicians and public managers.

To summarize: A number of studies on contractual governance have been conducted already. While a couple of these studies are normative and descriptive (notably Savas), a number of studies have presented theoretical models of contractual models by building on empirical evidence. This empirical evidence comes from in-depth case studies (Romzek and Johnston; Milward and Provan; Wegener; Bryntse), survey data (Hodge), and single case studies (Wallin; Johnson and Waltzer). A select number of general (text) books present fine judgments and valuable insights into the contracting process (Domberger; Cooper), as do a number of edited books on the subject (Johnson and Waltzer; Fortin and van Hassel).

SUMMARY

In this chapter we have examined the concepts of "contract" and "contractual governance." We have found a basic concept of a contract and an expanded interpretation of a contract. These were examined further as "hard" (classical and neoclassical, competitive) and "soft" (relational, negotiation) contracts. Stretching the notion of a soft contract enables us to point to a cooperative contract that takes the form of a genuine partnership. Furthermore, the behavioral assumptions of contracting were discussed, and we contrasted the logic of consequentiality (found in rational choice studies) with the logic of appropriateness (found in sociological institutional studies). Combining these features in a 2x2 table, we came up with the conditions for contractual governance.

The challenge for contractual governance is to balance between hard and soft contracts and different behavioral assumptions. When looking more in detail at the contract implementation and management process, several theoretical and empirical studies were examined. Building from Kettl's original insight into the nature of contractual governance, a number of studies have refined and expanded the model of contractual governance that will be used as a building block for the next chapter.

3

Contractual Governance

INTRODUCTION

In this chapter we introduce a conceptual framework for the following analyses of the processes of contracting. First, we want to give a thorough description of the contracting process; second, we look at ways to explain the course of the process. The questions are interrelated. The first gives us insight to elements internal to the process; how these different elements are handled will influence the course of the process. However, the course of the contracting process is also influenced by elements external to the process.

Contracting for services may be considered a public policy like any other policy initiated by government. The question is who gets what, when, and how. Public policy is often studied with a focus on the process, using some sort of model that divides the process into phases. One example of such a model is Brewer and DeLeon's (1983) six-phase model, consisting of the following phases: Initiation, Estimation, Selection, Implementation, Evaluation, and Termination. The policy in question can be analyzed by going through the different phases in the model. Such a model may be helpful in gaining an overall understanding of the process of contracting; more important, it underlines the political aspects of the process. However, it is too general to catch the specifics of a policy and in this case does not address key questions in relation to public service contracting. The models used in public policy analysis must be more specific to be helpful in analyzing contracting.

Fortunately, many others have suggested models that describe the process of contracting and offer key questions to be answered when contracting for public services. Some are analytical in their scope, while others are normative, "how to" publications that give guidelines for contracting. In the international literature, numerous models describing the process of contracting can be found. Savas (2000), National League of Cities (1997), Cohen (2001), and Kettl (1993) are examples of models trying to capture key features of the process of contracting.

Savas (2000, 175) lists 12 steps in contracting for services:

1. Consider the idea of contracting out.
2. Select the service.
3. Conduct a feasibility study.
4. Foster competition.
5. Request expression of interest or qualifications.
6. Plan the employee transition.
7. Prepare bid specifications.
8. Initiate a public relations campaign.
9. Engage in "managed competition."
10. Conduct a fair bidding process.
11. Evaluate the bids and award the contract.
12. Monitor, evaluate, and enforce contract performance.

Savas´s model taps several key aspects of the process. His model and his discussion of the steps is dominated by a very positive attitude toward contracting; he does not pay much attention to the downside of contracting.

The National League of Cities, in its publication "Thinking through the Privatization Option," gives its view on the contracting process. The foreword to the guide says that it "provides to municipal officials a context for decisions about delivering services and offers a systematic process encompassing practical steps and ethical considerations for making decisions about the option of privatization." Its focus is on the decision to contract out and less on the questions that arise after that decision. Consideration of the decision to contract out should go through the following questions: Should government be responsible for a given function? Is there a policy reason why government should perform the function? Is government currently successful at performing the function? Can government make the changes in-house needed to become more competitive? Answering "yes" to the first question and "no" to the rest, government should use outside resources to accomplish government ends. It is argued that a more structured approach to decisions about contracting can help to secure positive effects and avoid pitfalls (National League of Cities 1997, 3).

Cohen (2001) gives a strategic framework for making the privatization decision. The framework raises a number of questions government should answer when considering contracting. Again the emphasis is on the elements prior to the implementation of contracting, but it raises questions important to handling the contracting process on an ongoing basis.

Cohen includes the following 10 questions:

1. What are the goals of the program we are planning?
2. What are the tasks that must be performed to achieve the goals of the program?
3. Does government currently have the capacity to perform these tasks?
4. How measurable are the outputs and outcomes of the activities we are seeking to undertake?
5. How capital intensive is the activity?
6. How much risk is involved in performing this activity?
7. What is the impact if the activity is performed poorly?
8. Is there a competitive market for the activity we are considering privatizing?
9. What is the output expected from this activity?
10. What is the outcome or impact expected from this activity?

Cohen argues that the privatization decision involves not only the question of whether production is placed in one or another type of organization, but also a number of political, economic, social, technical, and ethical issues (Cohen 2001, 440). This argument supports the need to look at a broad set of factors in order to understand the process of contracting.

Romzek and Johnston (2002) give by their "preliminary model" a way to understand the implementation process. Furthermore, their analytical model attempts to explain variations in the effectiveness of the implementation and management of contracts. They point to seven factors that have a positive impact on contract implementation and management and three factors that have a negative impact. The positive factors include the level of competition among providers, resource adequacy, planning for performance measurement, training for contract managers, evaluation of contractor staffing capacity, evaluation of contractor financial management capacity, and theoretical rationale for reform. The negative factors are the political strength of client advocates, complexity of subcontractor relationships, and risk shifting to the contractor. Romzek and Johnston test their model by using five cases from Kansas. The test supports the model, explaining the variation in contract implementation and management.

Kettl's (1993) notion of the "smart buyer" can be used to characterize the process of contracting. A smart buyer must answer three questions. The government must consider "what to buy?", "whom to buy from?",

Figure 3.1   Analyzing the process of contracting.

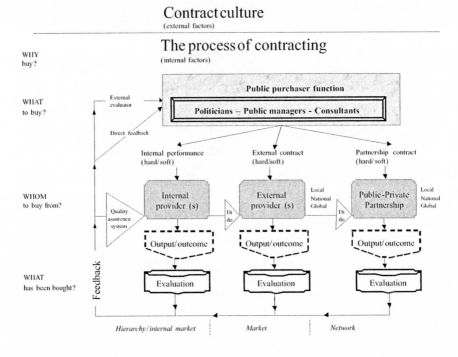

and "what has been bought?" These questions not only capture the key features of the contracting process but also allow one to address the complexity of the process.

The models just discussed have mostly a practical approach to contracting. Nevertheless, the insight gained from these models can be used to design an analytical framework for analyzing the process of contracting in different settings and different government systems.

To analyze the process of contracting we suggest a framework that includes both internal and external factors. Figure 3.1 illustrates the framework. Next we discuss the elements of the framework, starting with the internal factors describing the process and continuing with the external factors influencing the course of the process.

INTERNAL FACTORS

The internal factors are accounted for by extending Kettl's notion of the smart buyer at various points. Our aim is to combine the simplicity of Kettl's model with a more thorough discussion inspired by the models just presented. Whereas Kettl's "smart buyer" has its main focus on contracting out, we develop a model able to analyze both contracting out and internal contracting.

Inspired by Kettl, we ask four broad questions to capture the main characteristics of the contracting process.

1. Why buy? The purpose of the question is to understand the background of initiating a contracting process, the objectives sought by using contracting, and whether the decision to contract is guided by explicit theoretical considerations.
2. What to buy? As suggested by Kettl, the answer addresses resources allocated to the task that is being put up for contracting and the level of quality. Government must be able to define its goals and objectives independently of the one producing the good or service. In addition, we pay attention to the way governments organize themselves when using contracting and which actors influence the process.
3. Whom to buy from? This question concerns the criteria used when choosing among different suppliers. Does the government allow internal suppliers to put in bids, and how should they choose among the bids? When deciding whom to buy from, the government must also evaluate the supplier's capability to deliver the services at the requested level of quality and its ability to deliver data enabling the government to control the service delivered.
4. What has been bought? The government must control and evaluate whether suppliers have observed the terms of the contract. We also look at how government manages the contract during the period of the contract and how it organizes the control of external and internal suppliers.

Why Buy?

It is evident that many objectives and agendas are at stake when a government decides to contract for services. Which objectives have influenced the decision the most will without doubt influence the contracting process, including the organizational setup.

The decision to contract and privatize can be supported theoretically by economics-inspired theories, such as public choice theory. In brief, public choice theory argues that the lack of a profit motive will encourage public employees to maximize the size of the budget instead of maximizing the utility of the citizens (Hodge 2002, 20). In other words, by introducing competition into the public sector, a more effective public sector can be expected.

In his comprehensive study of contracting out, Hodge (2000, 25) lists four categories of motives: economic, political, consumer, and other.

Included among them are higher efficiency, increased competition, smaller government, reduced trade union power, consumer sovereignty, and decreased administrative burden from the state bureaucracy. Many of these objectives are echoed in Savas's list of 14 organization characteristics increasing the likelihood of contracting (2000, 111). His list includes factors like undermaintenance of facilities and equipment, multiple and conflicting goals, and theft and corruption.

The importance of the answer to the question "Why buy?" becomes evident when comparing the experiences from New Zealand and Denmark (Ejersbo and Greve 2002, 218). The use of contracting in New Zealand was driven by ideological motives and inspired by theoretical models like principal-agent theory and transaction cost economics. The result was a comprehensive reform process that introduced contracts in all branches of government, creating public enterprises later to be sold off, and reducing the number of public employees.

In contrast, the "Danish Model" can be characterized as pragmatic and lacking a theoretical point of departure. Relational (soft) contracts were not only a consequence but also an aim in themselves (Ejersbo and Greve 2002, 230). As a consequence, contracting is used selectively in the public sector and the use of contracts is only expanding slowly throughout the public sector. Contracting is used in combination with other management tools, not as the only tool or method.

It is difficult to argue that one motive to contract is better than another. Nevertheless, some objectives are more likely to be successful than others. Romzek and Johnston (2002, 7) point in their model of effective implementation to the importance of the theoretical integrity of the rationale for contracting reform. They argue that a flawed rationale will make implementation difficult.

What to Buy?

The public organization must decide which services should be under contract. This decision will be influenced by its motives for engaging in contracting. It can focus on tasks where efficiency gains are likely to occur, or on services experiencing difficulties that may obtain a satisfactory service level. The decision to contract out specific services can also be supported by theoretical considerations. By referring to transaction costs, Williamson argues that characteristics of a specific task or service can tell whether the task or service should be produced internally in the public sector or externally (Williamson 1975).

When the tasks or services subject to contracting are decided, following Kettl, the smart buyer must clarify the level of service and the resources to be allocated. This may sound easy, but it presumes information about possible service levels (also the current) and some knowledge about the production processes. Lack of information and knowledge may be a problem not only when tasks or services are not currently handled by the public organization but also when the tasks or services are already in-house. The clarifying of objectives demands organizational capacity and sufficient resources.

The local government can choose to make specific organizational arrangements involving certain groups of people when working out quality levels. A common recommendation is to create a purchaser-provider split (Lane 2000; Osborne and Gaebler 1993). The basic idea is to make a clear distinction between those who decide on the level of quality and resources allocated and those who will produce the good or service. This type of arrangement is important when contracting involves parts of the public organization as producers.

Government may also set up a new section handling all questions and tasks in connection with contracting and building an expertise among personnel in the organization. Others may use the existing organization and maybe add expertise from outside the organization. Depending on the general organizational arrangement, different levels of the organization may be involved in decisions on quality and resources. In some cases the decision will be lifted to the political level and involve elected officials not only in a formal way but as active participants. In other cases it is left to the administration to make the formal decision.

Whom to Buy From?

"Who to buy from" concerns the market structure and addresses issues like the number of companies operating in the market, the level of competition, and the possibility of negotiating special agreements between buyer and seller. A precondition for contracting out is the presence of a market. If opportunities to contract out are to be utilized, a minimum degree of competition should be present (Savas 2000). In other words, a public monopoly should not be replaced by a private monopoly, or nothing has been gained.

In microeconomic theory, in a perfect competitive market there are a large number of firms and free movement of firms and buyers in and out of the market, and firms and buyers have a perfect knowledge of the prices of products (Truett and Truett 1984, 191). Translating these characteristics to a situation of contracting, a large number of possible service providers can be identified. The competition between different firms has as a consequence that prices are at the lowest possible level. If prices were too high, the possibility of making a profit would attract new firms, forcing the price down. As a consequence, local governments will be able to make savings compared to delivering the service themselves. This theoretical market situation is often the assumption behind contracting out, but it is seldom the case, in reality.

When the market is characterized by oligopoly, there are only a few firms or firms dominating other firms. Firms are aware of their mutual interdependence, and it is difficult to enter the market (Truett and Truett 1984, 246). The limited number of firms and the barriers to entering the market can result in too-high prices. In a market characterized by oligopoly, local governments may be facing cartels, where firms in the market have agreed on a fixed price—a price above the price in a perfect competitive market. In addition, local governments may end up being dependent upon a few dominant firms to deliver the service.

Monopoly is the worst-case scenario for local governments when contracting out services (Truett and Truett 1984, 207). In a situation with monopoly on the market, contracting out means changing from a public to a private monopoly, and the possible gains from contracting out will disappear.

A perfect competitive market is seldom found. More often, government is facing a situation of oligopoly or monopoly. Market imperfections such as oligopoly and monopoly make it difficult for governments to know from whom to buy (Kettl 1993, 181). In relation to many services and goods traditionally delivered by public organizations, a fully competitive market does not exist. Looking at a number of case studies of contracting, it becomes evident how market imperfections vary between different sectors. In some cases, the bidding process involves a large number companies and real competition, while other attempts to contract out fail due to lack of potential bidders and competition.

Local governments can use different strategies to create a market and secure more competition. Some obstacles to competition may be found within the organization itself. Bureaucratic procedures may cause potential bidders to abandon the process. Hence, governments must make it easy for private companies to participate in order to increase competition. Savas (2000) suggests dividing the contract into smaller pieces either geographically or functionally. He also mentions the need to give sufficient information to bidders, to let more than one single bidder be successful, and to spread the contracts over several years in order to let losers from the first round be successful in a following round of bids. These strategies may be helpful, but creating competition is difficult and no single strategy will solve the problem of a lack of competition.

If the objective is less government but not necessarily private companies, letting a nonprofit organization carry out the task may be a possibility (Salamon 1995; Light 2000). Both in the United States and Scandinavia, nonprofit organizations have had a place in providing welfare services. Nonprofit organizations in the United States are more oriented toward service production and put less emphasis on membership and democratic influence (Eikås and Selle 2000, 40).

Local government can also allow in-house bids to participate in the bidding process. This strategy demands a clear purchaser-provider split within the public organization, and it may keep production in-house. If the objective is to let private companies in on producing public services, government should be careful allowing in-house bids. If the strategy is higher efficiency and cost reduction, Hodge (2000, 119) shows that the most important factor is competition, not whether the production is placed in a public or private organization.

Experiences from Danish local government show that local governments are reluctant to allow in-house bids (Kommunernes Landsforening 2000), while cases from U.S. local governments indicate in-house bids to be more common.

Besides looking at the price of the service, when deciding on a provider, local governments must also evaluate the capacity of the supplier to deliver both the product and a support system surrounding production. Romzek and Johnston's (2002) model of effective implementation emphasizes the importance of provider capacity. Without sufficient staffing capacity and financial management by the contractor, governments will not be able to get services delivered correctly.

Many of the considerations presented have relevance for contracting out and internal contracting alike. When it comes to the question of "whom to buy from," the relevance is less obvious. For most services it is difficult to imagine an internal market within a local government. The introduction to internal contracting may be seen as a preparation to contracting out at a later stage. It can be an opportunity for departments or sections to prepare the organization to compete and to make the organization more aware of strengths and weaknesses. Alternatively, internal contracting can be viewed as a threat to departments not performing up to standard that they may lose tasks to outside producers in a later contracting process with outside bidders. From this point of view, internal contracting may not include a choice among providers initially, but it can be a first stage for introducing competition between public and private providers.

What Has Been Bought?

What has been bought involves questions of control, audit, and accountability. Control means the immediate control to ensure that objectives are met according to the contractual obligations. Auditing, by no means a well-defined concept, now covers aspects other than the examination of financial statements (Flint 1998). Auditing is the act of "going through the books" and making sure that money is spent wisely (financial audit) and that value is obtained for the money (administrative or managerial audit). With the rise of new public management (NPM) and performance-based management, the latter type of audit has attracted a great deal of attention. It is also suggested that auditing should be understood as an idea, a way of signaling control and values (Power 1994). Accountability is the act of "holding someone to account" for a particular action or decision. The concept of accountability has been explored and defined more thoroughly as involving hierarchical, legal, political, and professional meanings (Romzek 1998). The relationships among these three practices are hard to establish. However, it seems likely that accountability is somewhat more important than the two others, and that you have to get "control" and "audit" right before anyone can be held to account proper.

Answering the question "what has been bought" is by no means an easy task. From the literature on evaluation we know how difficult it is to secure formal evaluations of programs or policies. We can expect the same kind of difficulties when it comes to contracts. When a local government has a hard time finding out what to buy, it will also find it difficult to evaluate the quality.

Governments can make evaluation easier by managing the contracts properly during the contracting period. In the "classical" contract all eventualities and potential problems are handled before the contract is signed. However, not all tasks and services in the public sector can be fitted into the classical contract. The public sector especially deals with "wicked" problems (Harmon and Mayer 1986). Wicked problems are problems without a clear-cut solution, as opposed to "tame" problems whose solutions are easier to find. Construction projects, solid waste collection, and street cleaning are examples of tame problems. We know from several studies of contracting that even these types of services create several problems during the period of the contract. Then it is not difficult to imagine the difficulties that can be expected when it comes to "wicked" problems in the social services. As a consequence, attention must be paid to the interaction between the contracting parties during the period of the contract and how public organizations manage their contracts.

Different actors can be involved in the evaluation (covering control, audition, and accountability). The providers can be a vital part in evaluating the services delivered. They may not be the only part in the evaluation process, but they can supply important information. Often it is specified in the contract that the provider must document the quality of the services. The provider's own quality management systems can be important factors in evaluating and securing the quality of the services. The buyer must be cautious if too great a part of the evaluation process is handed over to the provider and if the buyer relies on the provider to give vital information about the quality of the services. On the other hand, the buyer must also avoid practicing micromanagement (Savas 2000).

EXTERNAL FACTORS

Taking institutional arrangements into account is at the very heart of comparative studies. Various comparative studies of contracting suggest different sets of variables to capture national characteristics.

The level of analysis in the models previously discussed has been on the organizational level. The models look at different features and questions organizations must address when contracting. The answers to these questions will influence the course of the process. However, the course of the contracting process is also influenced by factors outside the single organization. As Cooper (2003) puts it, "A brief reconsideration of the rise of the contract state tells us a good deal about why the current system looks and functions as it does" (16). This quote also points to the importance of the historical dimension. The use of contracts has a history, which influences current processes of contracting. To fully understand the factors influencing the course of the process, it is necessary to develop an analytical framework taking both internal and external factors into account.

The external factors are summarized in the term "contract culture." It covers the institutional setup surrounding the process of contracting. In a comparative study the institutional setup or contract culture is of special interest. By looking at contracting in different contract cultures, we can get a much better understanding of the both the contractual process and the importance of the institutional setup.

Other comparative studies of contracting have suggested ways to capture the national/institutional characteristics. Cassell's (2002) study of disinvestment in Germany and the United States includes *systems of governance* besides factors under the control of specific actors or organizations. In Cassell's work, systems of governance include beliefs and attitudes about the state and policy-making institutions, beliefs and attitudes about markets and economic regulatory structures, and beliefs and attitudes about the bureaucracy and bureaucratic structures. By including systems of governance, he looks "outward to take stock of how a public bureaucracy's administrative structures and practices conform to the larger or 'macro' system of governance specific to a country" (Cassell 2002, 14).

Bryntse (2000) studies contracting out in Sweden, Germany, and England. She develops a framework that includes internal as well as external factors, using three broad sets of categories. One category focuses on organization-related explanations, another category focuses on activity-related explanations, and a third category looks at nation-related explanations. Our interest is mainly on the last category. The nation-related explanations include societal system, legislation and government policy, business culture, and voluntary regulation.

Along the same lines as Cassell and Bryntse, we use "contract culture" to capture factors outside the control of the single organization and factors linked to national characteristics. The concept looks specifically at the formal and informal rules and attitudes surrounding the process of contracting. Formal rules include regulation of competition and tendering procedures and of public sector activities in general. The informal rules and attitudes surrounding contracting attempt to describe how contracting is perceived in the public sector and among the public, how accepted the use of contracting is among public sector organizations, and how public-private interaction is perceived and placed in the political debate.

We suggest the following elements to describe the contract culture:

- National/international legislation—the regulatory praxis
- The history of contracting in the public sector
- The nature and level of public-private interaction
- The political debate surrounding contracting
- Attitudes toward contracting—in the public sector and among the public

The Regulatory Praxis

The national and international legislation surrounding the process gives the formal framework for contracting services. Legislation (contract law, etc.) will influence the process. However, it is important to notice the latitude left to the parties to shape the agreement and decide how it will be operated (Cooper 2003, 13).

In the United States, national legislation influences the process, but state-specific legislation will be important as well.

In the Scandinavian case, European Union legislation demands an open bidding process when the cost of construction projects exceeds a certain level. In principle, the bidding process should be open not only to national companies, but to companies in all the EU member states. The legislation regulates in a simple way when public organizations must engage in an open bidding process. The EU legislation is targeted at construction projects and not at general public services.

National legislation is important as well. In 2002 the Danish parliament passed legislation giving private companies the right to challenge the price of all local government services. The local government must calculate the cost of the service in question when carried out by the local government and let the private company challenge the price calculated. The local council then has the opportunity to choose the cheapest form of production. The private companies' right to challenge the cost of local government services obviously influences local governments' decisions on what to buy; the decision-making authority more or less taken out of the hands of local government and placed in the hands of private companies.

History

Specific contracting processes in a state or local government are always part of a history—a history of contracting in the public sector, formed by specific events or lines of events that have taken place outside the organization but can be used as points of reference when contracting is discussed. They can be well-known cases such as Indianapolis or San Diego, as U.S. examples, or Farum, as a Scandinavian example. It may include spectacular debates in national or state parliaments in connection with passing new legislation. Or it can be a history of several unsuccessful attempts to increase the level of services contracted out, or high-profile case stories showing how successful contracting out public services can be. All such events are part of a specific national history of contracting, which will influence how the process of contracting is carried out in a specific organization.

The Nature of Public-Private Interaction

Looking at the nature and level of public-private interaction is a way to tap the maturity of a contracting culture. In a context of a large public sector with limited experience with contracting, the process will be trial and error in each organization using contracting. The level of experience and learning between organizations is limited, and basic knowledge has to be established each time a public organization starts a process of contracting out services. In such a situation the process has to be designed over again each time an organization decides to use contracting. Knowledge of contracting is scattered across sectors and types of services. Knowledge may exist in specific areas or around specific types of services, but knowledge general enough to cut across sectors has not been established.

In the context of a smaller public sector with extensive experience with contracting and cooperation between public sector organizations and private companies, a common knowledge across sectors and types of services can be established. Due to long experience, standard procedures and well-tested ways to handle the process are available to organizations working with contracting. It is not necessary for organizations to develop new procedures or design a new process. They can draw from a common pool of experience.

The Political Debate

The political debate surrounding contracting sends signals to public sector organizations on how they ought to handle contracting. The influence on the process of contracting is mostly indirect as is the case with other aspects of the contract culture. Nevertheless, signals from government or strong parties in parliament can have as much impact as legislation. Local governments and other organizations may view such statements as threats. If public organizations do start acting in a specific way, parliament will turn to legislation to make organizations act according to political viewpoints.

Attitudes toward Contracting

Depending on public attitudes toward interaction between the public sector and private companies, the process of contracting can be slowed down or speeded up. In a situation with general mistrust of corporations between public and private organizations, policy makers will be more hesitant to engage in contracting. This type of situation will focus much more attention on formal procedures and the evaluation of contracted services.

SUMMARY

In this chapter we present a framework for understanding the course of the process of contracting. We argue that such an analysis must include a thorough description of not only internal aspects of the process but also external aspects. Our description of the internal aspects uses Kettl's notion of "the smart buyer" as a point of departure and expands it by including insights from other descriptions of the contracting process. Accordingly, the process of contracting is described by the following four questions: Why buy? What to buy? Whom to buy from? What has been bought? To capture the external aspects, we introduce the concept *contract culture*. Contract culture covers elements such as the regulatory praxis, the history of contracting in the public sector, the nature and level of public-private interaction, the political debate surrounding contracting, and attitudes toward contracting.

4

Policy Change and Learning in Contracting Out

INTRODUCTION

Contracting out has been on the political and administrative agenda for two decades. Who has been promoting the contracting idea? Who has been against the contracting idea? How have attitudes of the main players toward contracting out changed? Which factors have influenced the development of contracting out? Have the participants in the debate over contracting learned something along the way?

Identifying proponents and opponents of contracting has not been done in a systematic way in the literature. The discussion on contracting has focused on organizational design questions, accountability questions, and output/outcome questions. DeHoog (1984) was an early proponent of the need to look at the contracting process, stating that "it is time that public administrationists go beyond the economists' simple cost comparisons of public versus private production of services to examine contracting out process, including its political, administrative, and performance components." The idea was put forward that contracting should be understood in a self-referential way (Miller and Simmons 1998) where contracting out is interpreted as a "fraud," which bears no reference to real-life administrative experience. This last type of claim is unsubstantiated by research. But there is a need to pay closer attention to how contracting has developed politically.

Second, there is a need to find out which factors have influenced the development of contracting out. Is it factors like the economy or, in Europe, European Union legislation? Or is the factor pushing contracting out still ideological, as the critics have claimed? Third, there is a need to find out if the actors engage in a meaningful exchange of views and knowledge in order to learn how to improve policy on contracting out. Otherwise, it is just an ideological struggle.

This chapter addresses three questions: How does contracting get onto the political agenda? How does the change in policy of contracting out take place? Do participants in the policy process engage in learning from contracting out policy and practice?

One constructive theoretical framework for answering these questions is found in the Advocacy Coalition Framework (ACF) proposed by Sabatier and Jenkins-Smith (1993, 1999; Sabatier 1998). Their research agenda focuses on actors pursuing policy change, the external factors surrounding change processes, and the conditions for policy learning to take place.

The empirical basis for the chapter is a database constructed to trace the Danish debate on contracting in the media in the period 1995–2000. We will elaborate on the relevance for the American debate.

The chapter is divided into the following parts. The first section after this introduction explains the theoretical perspective of the ACF and establishes three hypotheses from that perspective. The second part of the chapter briefly explains the method employed. The third part of the chapter analyzes the empirical results from the database. The fourth part discusses the results. The concluding part sums up the main findings of the agenda question, puts them in perspective, and discusses future initiatives to be taken in this kind of research.

THE ADVOCACY COALITION FRAMEWORK
APPLIED TO CONTRACTING POLICY

One approach that has been particularly strong in recent years in public policy analysis is the work on the Advocacy Coalition Framework (ACF) by Sabatier and Jenkins-Smith (1993, 1999). An advocacy coalition is defined as "people from a variety of positions, elected and agency officials, interest group leaders, researchers who share a particular belief system, and who show a non-trivial degree of coordinated behavior over time" (Sabatier and Jenkins-Smith, 1993).

The ACF evolved from discontent with the implementation literature. There is a clear connection with much of the policy network literature (Rhodes 1997; Kickert, Klijn, and Koppenjan 1997). They both focus on subsystems of actors, the relationships between actors, and the borders of the network from other policy networks. There are coexisting networks, but they are stable in their commitment to their values. But the ACF presents a view of a dynamic network and is thereby able to explain change. The reasons are external shocks, change in personnel, and policy learning. The policy network approach has been criticized for having inadequate theory on policy change.

The objective of the ACF is to "provide a coherent understanding of the major factors and processes affecting the overall policy process—including problem definition, policy formation, implementation, and revision in a specific policy domain—over periods of a decade or more" (Sabatier 1998, 98). The ACF makes a number of assumptions, which Sabatier has summarized: First, technical information plays an unrecognized role in the policy process. Technical information is produced by many sources and feeds into the policy-makers' decision sphere. Second, a time span of 10 years is needed in order to grasp the development in the policy process. Too often, policy studies have had a short time frame and so have had difficulty in reviewing the output or outcome. Third, the policy subsystem is judged the "most useful unit of analysis." Instead of focusing on a single organization, the policy subsystem is the preferred unit. Fourth, the participants in the policy process are not as predetermined as in usual interest group explanations. The participants include, of course, politicians in political parties and interest groups. Added to that are private sector companies and nonprofit organizations. But the participants can also be public managers, journalists, and researchers. In broadening the spectrum of participants, the ACF goes beyond the corporatist image that has clung to the more traditional policy network approach. Fifth, a learning process is possible. Actors are assumed to be willing and able to change their policy if sufficient evidence is presented.

The actors' belief systems are important to the ACF. The belief systems are divided into three belief types. The first one is "deep core beliefs," which are deeply held and cannot be changed easily. Changing a deep core belief is akin to religious conversion. The second type of belief system is "policy core beliefs." Actors have some particular perspectives that form their policy views and they can be changed under certain circumstances. The third type of belief system is called "secondary aspects." Actors are here willing and able to change their attitudes after analytical debates and discussions. Policy learning takes place when secondary or core beliefs change. The participants know themselves when they are learning and when they are not learning.

The ACF seems particularly well suited to analyzing the policy process of contracting out. First, there is a huge amount of technical information related to contracting out procedures. Second, contracting out has been on the agenda since the mid-1980s, picking up in the 1990s. Third, the local government service to be contracted out is the focus point for the policy subsystem engaged in contracting out policy, which consists of a number of different actors. Fourth, these actors come from a variety of places, and they include politicians, local governments, public managers, interest groups, and unions as well as journalists and researchers. Fifth, there is an official willingness to produce more knowledge on the theory and practice of contracting out and an indication that the knowledge produced will be put to use and be fed back into the policy process and decision making.

The ACF has been criticized for not producing anything radically new from the implementation literature (deLeon 1999) and for being overly sophisticated for its own good (too many variables). Sabatier and Jenkins-Smith are too obsessed with coalitions' attitudes and cannot explain changes in policy, according to Winter (1994). However, few researchers have done as much as Sabatier and Jenkins-Smith to include a wide variety and number of actors and examine how policy experience is actually learned from and changed.

The ACF framework has developed a number of hypotheses that are tested in empirical research (Sabatier and Jenkins-Smith, 1999, for the latest edition). For the contracting policy, we have formulated three hypotheses which are tested on our empirical data.

Hypothesis one concerns the composition of advocacy coalitions: There exist at least two competing contracting out advocacy coalitions in Denmark. There is an ideological conflict, in which each coalition has a different deep core belief. The lineup of allies and opponents of contracting out have been stable in Denmark throughout the 1990s, but there are policy brokers (government ministries) between different views.

Hypothesis two concerns policy change: Policy change takes place as a result of changes both in the external environment of the economy and in European Union directives on contracting out—and through internal factors such as ideologically motivated policies.

Hypothesis three concerns policy learning: Policy-oriented learning in contracting out happens when coalitions alter or revise their belief systems. Policy learning occurs in Denmark because two relatively stable coalitions engage in ongoing debates, based on technical information through reports and the like. The venues for this debate include the media as well as professional forums (meetings, workshops, conferences).

METHOD

We constructed a database on advocacy coalition behavior in Denmark for the period of 1995 to 2000. The data was compiled from two primary sources. The first was a national newspaper in Denmark called *Berlingske Tidende*. The paper has a conservative outlook, but it is a broadsheet paper representative of news coverage in Denmark. The other broadsheet papers are *Jyllands-Posten* and *Politiken*. The second source is the biweekly journal *Danske Kommuner*, published by the Danish National Association for Local Government. The journal covers news stories concerning Denmark's 275 local governments.

A search for the keywords "contracting" and "contracting out" was conducted for the whole period. The sample contains 433 articles in *Berlingske Tidende* and 101 articles in *Danske Kommuner*, which represents the period of research, 1995–2000. However, the following analysis is based on the 633 different actors' attitudes, which comes to 2,707 attitudes (N = 2,707). The attitudes, not the articles, are the focus of this research.

The articles were then coded by our research assistant and processed into the database. The items registered were the cases and the actors. An actor is here an organization, a person, an association, or a political party. The research assistant assigned an initial value to each actor. As a point of departure for comparing the actors' attitudes toward contracting out, each actor was given a deep-core belief following the traditional right–left scale on political beliefs. However, some actors could not be categorized on this scale, and these actors were given a broker code/belief. This value assignment was done on the basis of a traditional left-right scale on political beliefs.

THE RESULTS

Issues

The number of cases identified was 52. Of these 52 cases, 10 cases had entries of "10" or over (Table 4.1). 167 entries were outside of any case. One case ("Social Democratic Party and contracting out") dominated the picture with 46 entries. The follow-up case ("The Liberal Party and the proposal of mandatory contracting out") had 20 entries. This was followed by two cases with 18 entries each ("Nurses" and "the bus company Ri-bus in Esbjerg Municipality." One case ("Busses and trains") had 16 entries, while the next case ("Hilden and the Hackers") had 14 entries. "ISS Company and Sweden" followed with 13 entries.

Six of the top 10 cases concerned political initiatives regarding contracting out. Contracting out has been controversial for the Social Democratic Party, which was also the party in government from 1993 to 2001. The party was divided with regard to contracting out. Many unions opposed it. The leading members of the party were modestly in favor of contracting out. Another case, called "Hilden and the Hackers" after its spokesperson Jytte Hilden, involves controversies around the annual party meeting in 1997, where a proposal was made for more use of contracting out by four leading social democrats, including a former chairman of the Social

TABLE 4.1

Issues in the Policy Debate on Contracting Out Public Services in 1995–2000

Issue	1995	1996	1997	1998	1999	2000	Total	%
Articles without any specific issue	19	27	33	29	35	24	167	31%
The Social Democratic Party and contracting out		10		18	14	4	46	9%
Proposal for compulsory contracting out in local government by the Liberal Party			13	2	3	2	20	4%
The bus company Ri-bus in Esbjerg municipality	15	2	1				18	3%
Nurses		9			2	7	18	3%
Busses and trains	1	3	4	4	2	2	`16	3%
Debate paper, presented by a group of social democrats, named "Hilden & the Hackers"		14					14	3%
ISS Company and Sweden			12	1			13	2%
The Liberal Party and contracting out		1		4	7		12	2%
Lack of contracting out in the federal government	4		1		1	4	10	2%
Election	1	1	6	1		1	10	2%

Note: The total number of issues was 52. Values entered are the number of articles in the sample in each year in each issue. The percentage is calculated by dividing the *Total* number by the total number of articles in the sample (534).

Democratic Youth Division and top union brass. The initiative was rejected by the members who participated in the annual party meeting. The other cases involves the party in opposition in the 1990s: The Liberal Party proposed making the tendering process compulsory for tasks worth more than 500.000 DKK. This was rejected by the government, but also by many local chapters of the Liberal Party itself.

Four of the top 10 cases concerned controversies in specific empirical cases. The first was the contracting out of a bus service in Ribe County in Denmark in the spring of 1995 that the unions opposed heavily. Strikes went on for more than a year because of allegedly bad wage and work conditions with the new company, Ri-bus, that had won the contract for providing bus service to the city. The second case concerns the work conditions for nurses at a home for elderly care in the town of Horsholm. The third case is a broad one concerning contracting out of bus and train service. The fourth case is about the Danish-based global company, ISS, that won a contract for elderly care in Solna in Sweden, but had to give up providing the service after malpractice was found in the elderly care home. More than 500 million DKK was wiped off ISS shareholding in just one day because of the bad news. The local government in Sweden later admitted that they had not prepared the contract and the takeover of the service professionally enough.

TABLE 4.2
Groups of Actors in the Policy Debate on Contracting Out

Groups of actors	1995	1996	1997	1998	1999	2000	Total	%
Socialist parliamentary parties and politicians	55	171	42	136	89	45	538	23%
Conservative-liberal parliamentary parties and politicians	41	97	62	67	49	36	352	15%
Local conservative-liberal parties and politicians	35	29	65	37	56	24	246	10%
Employees	34	38	23	33	53	15	196	8%
Private companies	19	33	38	28	22	19	159	7%
Local socialist parties and politicians	7	31	21	26	23	14	122	5%
Foreigners	11	23	28	18	16	11	107	5%
Danish National Association for Local Government and the County Association	16	15	23	12	14	26	106	4%
Public managers, civil servants, and bureaucrats	15	16	17	10	16	16	90	4%
Contracting out committees	10	10	10	10	12	19	71	3%
Public enterprises	15	16	15	11	5	4	66	3%
Consultants	16	8	11	6	11	7	59	2%
Not specified political institutions	10	18	17	3	3	6	57	2%
Researchers	6	16	7	12	6	5	52	2%
Others	3	13	13	5	10	4	48	2%
Employers	12	13	9	1	8	2	45	2%
Public regulatory organizations	7	7	4	3	9	12	42	2%
Journalists	2	1	3	1	1		8	0%

Note: The numbers are not equivalent to the number of articles because more than one actor has been covered in some articles.

Actors

The number of actors participating in the discourse was an astonishing 633 during the course of the period 1995–2000. The groups of actors were the following (in order of appearance in the debate): socialist parliamentary parties, conservative-liberal parliamentary parties, local conservative and liberal political parties, employees, private companies, local socialist political parties, public managers, foreigners, Danish National Association for Local Government, public regulatory organizations, other political-administrative organizations, researchers, employers, others, consultants, public enterprises, contracting out committees, voluntary nonprofit organizations, interest groups, and journalists (Table 4.2).

Type of Tasks Contracted Out Debated in the Period

The tasks that were discussed varied. "General production" topped the list, followed by elder care, softer welfare care, transportation, technical areas, other, child care, cleaning and maintenance, administration, human social services, public authority services, and primary schools (Table 4.3).

The composition of the list is not surprising, given the attention that these cases have received in the public debate. Contracting for human and

TABLE 4.3
Public Services Mentioned in the Contracting Out Policy Debate

Type of Service	1995	1996	1997	1998	1999	2000	Total	%
General production	31	29	34	21	30	25	170	32%
Elderly care	15	41	15	11	23	16	121	23%
Softer welfare care	2	4	4	28	8	9	55	10%
Transportation	14	7	6	9	5	3	44	8%
Technical areas	5	10	5	11	8	1	40	7%
Other	2	4	9	7	8	2	32	6%
Child care	2		5	1	6	6	20	4%
Cleaning and maintenance		2	6		9	2	19	4%
Administrative services		2	3	5	5	3	18	3%
Human social services			1		2	5	8	1%
Public authority services			3			2	5	1%
Education			2				2	0%

Note: Percentages are calculated by dividing the Total number by the number of articles in the sample (534). Values are the number of articles in the sample.

social services has been the most controversial and the most visible type of services added to the list of tasks to be contracted out. Transportation is often also controversial because transportation's effect can immediately be read from peoples' responses. Child care has also been a center of attention, although there are not many cases of child care being contracted out. The most visible have been a kindergarten run by ISS in Skovbo local government and a kindergarten run by Jydsk Rengoring (which merged with ISS) in Assens on the island of Funen. The city of Copenhagen also contracted out a child care facility in the year 2000. Cleaning and maintenance has long been on the list for tasks that are contracted out and is repeatedly found on the lists provided by the 2000 Danish National Association of Local Government survey and the 1997 survey done by PLS and the Ministry of the Interior. Administration is a new task added to the list. It was introduced in the local government of Farum in North Sealand, which contracted out some of its tasks to Deloitte and Touche. Three other local governments, including Hoje Taastrup, examined the case for contracting out administrative tasks, but remained modestly interested. Social tasks have not been contracted out to private companies in a big way, but most relate to informal understandings with nonprofit organizations. Tasks involving the use of public authority are an ongoing and controversial question. The official line the government takes is that public authority cannot be contracted out. However, this is being challenged constantly—often by the government itself in actual practice.

Technical Information

The kind of technical information used was also examined (Table 4.4). Technical information here means information about how con-

TABLE 4.4
Types of Technical Information on Contracting Out

Type of technical reports	Reports on employee rights and duties	Reports on experiences with contracting out	Reports with guidelines and practical steps	Reports as policy papers and campaign papers
Published by	Trade unions	Government departments and local government organizations	Consultants (at the suggestion of government)	Governments, interest groups, trade unions

tracting out can be implemented in practice. It includes reports published by, for example, trade unions, governments, consultants, and interest groups.

In the European Union, legislation has been discussed on several occasions, including the Liberal Party's proposal to make tendering mandatory for all local governments. Legislation here also includes references to European Union directives and planned changes in directives. There are also discussions on changes to the regulations that are law now. For example, a rule forbids the use of private personal care assistants, as the law states they should be publicly employed. This has caused controversy and led to a lengthy exchange of views—including lawyers' responses—between the local government of Graested-Gilleleje and the Ministry of the Interior.

Both central and local government have made use of consultants' reports to clarify matters and to provide overview to the contracting out debate. Among the most important consultancy reports, we can mention PLS report for the Ministry of the Interior in 1997, PLS report for the Ministry of Finance in 2000, PLS report for the State Council for Contracting Out, and COWI's report for the Ministry of Industry and Commerce in 2001.

Technical information is also supplied in rulings from the Danish Complaints Council for Tenders and from court rulings about employee conditions and rights.

Both central and local government have issued reports in addition to the reports they order from consultancy firms. The Ministry of Finance has written about contracting and partnership in the annual finance report of 1999 and has mentioned contracting out in the reports on More Freedom of Choice in public services, also in 1999.

The intensity of the debate period is interesting to look at. The contracting issue appears regularly in the public discussion as is recorded from the two sources used here (Table 4.5). There is no sign that the debate on contracting is finishing. Contracting discussions are linked to the cases reported (Table 4.6). Both coalitions continue to engage themselves in the

TABLE 4.5
Profile of the Policy Debate: Number of Articles

Source	1995	1996	1997	1998	1999	2000
Belingske Tidende	51	85	76	79	90	52
Danske Kommuner	20	14	17	14	14	22

Note: The values are the number of articles in each year

TABLE 4.6
Profile of the Policy Debate: Participation Percentages from Different Coalitions

Coalition	1995	1996	1997	1998	1999	2000
Anti–contracting out coalition	36%	46%	26%	49%	41%	31%
Broker	12%	9%	11%	8%	10%	19%
Pro–contracting out coalition	45%	36%	49%	37%	43%	44%
Unknown (not in any coalition or broker)	7%	9%	14%	6%	6%	7%

Note: The values are the number of actors in all the articles, and not the number of articles.

debate (Table 4.7). Contracting out comes on the agenda as a result of a deliberate political attempt to place it there. Or contracting out comes onto the agenda as some kind of controversy emerges, be it ISS and Sweden, Farum's attempt to contract out new tasks, or employees who feel they are not treated right.

Learning took place, but perhaps not as expected (Bjørn-Andersen, 2002). The conditions for learning appear to be met, but there is no convergence in attitudes between the two coalitions. A lesser convergence takes place because the anti–contracting out coalition becomes more positive in its attitudes toward contracting out. But there is still disagreement between the two coalitions. If that is to be changed, the conditions for learning must be changed, for example, by making the debate less ideological. To make the debate less ideological, technical information must be used and improved, for example, through national learning centers, such as an Internet portal on contracting out issues.

TABLE 4.7
The Coalitions' Attitudes toward Contracting Out

Coalition	1995	1996	1997	1998	1999	2000
Anti–contracting out coalition	0.40	0.39	0.58	0.61	0.58	0.55
Broker	0.62	0.65	0.72	0.80	0.73	0.62
Pro–contracting out coalition	0.80	0.94	0.86	0.92	0.97	0.93

Note: The value 1 is equivalent to a positive attitude; the value 0 is equivalent to a negative attitude.

Summing Up

From the evidence presented here, we can conclude, first, that contracting out has been consistently on the political-administrative agenda throughout the period studied. There is no reason to believe that contracting out will go away as an issue. Second, contracting out is debated specifically around a number of cases that dominate the debate for a while. Technical information has played a minor role in substantiating claims about or against contracting out. Change is connected to the outcome of these case deliberations. Specific actors push for change in contracting out, and mostly these initiatives come from political parties or central or local government. This makes up the advocacy coalition in favor of contracting out. These initiatives are opposed by another advocacy coalition. When cases are not linked to political initiatives, there is an open debate about the merits and the negative consequences. As these cases tend to pop up as surprises, they get debated hotly ("ISS and Sweden" being an example).

The initiatives are not specifically linked to external factors such as European Union directives or the state of the economy. Rather, the argument tends to be about more freedom of choice of public services and an improved quality of services. Third, there has been some movement in attitudes during the period. One advocacy coalition that has been skeptical toward contracting out is becoming more moderate or less critical of contracting out. The pro–contracting out advocacy coalition has not showed any sign of changing its attitudes, in the sense of modifying its views, but has remained a steadfast proponent of contracting out. This does not mean that it has not picked up new ideas about how to improve the contracting out process, only that it has not shown any sign of taking notice of the skeptical coalition.

DISCUSSION

In this section, we discuss the implications of the results reported in the last section and relate them to the three hypotheses introduced in the beginning of the chapter. First of all, what kinds of advocacy coalitions exist? And who are the brokers and what role do they perform? Second, how have the contracting processes and procedures changed during the period? Third, what constitutes learning in contracting out?

It seems probable that there are not only two advocacy coalitions, as first assumed, but a number of advocacy coalitions. From the material, we can identify at least four different groupings.

The first coalition is the radical reform coalition, which consists of innovative local governments and aggressive, reform-minded politicians. This group actively advocates for more contracting out. They are not afraid to take chances. They are ready to challenge official authorities. They have links with outside organizations such as the Cities of Tomorrow network in which Farum has participated. They may have the support of a few dedicated journalists, and a few researchers. Some interest groups as well as a small number of firms belong to this category.

The second coalition consists of modest reformers. They are interested in reform, but they see contracting out more as a tool than as a weapon to challenge the public sector. In this group, we find a number of local governments, including individual mayors, reform-minded politicians from the Liberal Party, the Social Democratic Party, and the Socialist People's Party (the mayor of Vejle), and a handful of private companies. We can also include a number of researchers from the universities as well as a number of journalists, and a number of consultancy firms. This is perhaps the biggest coalition.

The third coalition consists of the mildly skeptical. In this group, we find many of the trade unions, a number of local governments, journalists, and a few researchers. This group has been strong, but is perhaps not so strong anymore.

The fourth coalition consists of the radical opponents. This group consists of political parties on the far left, some trade unions, and selected journalists. We do not find any researchers here. This group is perhaps not so strong, and has never been very strong.

Who are the brokers? The brokers are mostly the ministries, the Danish National Association for Local Government, and some researchers and consultancy firms. The brokers hold meetings when new reports are drafted. The brokers are found in local governments that just want to get on with the work and do not care whether the service is provided by a public organization or a private organization.

Importantly, some organizations lead a double life, being members of advocacy coalitions and being brokers. The Ministry of Finance has long advocated more contracting out, which puts it in the modest reformers group. At the same time, the Ministry of Finance is responsible for providing information that all actors will recognize as valid technical information, which puts it in a broker position. The same goes for the Danish National Association of Local Governments.

The biggest groups are the modest reformers and the modest skeptics. Perhaps it is not so surprising that we found that learning has taken place between opponents and proponents. The movement has gone from the modest skeptics toward the group of the modest reformers. But it is not likely that the modest skeptics have gone all the way, to become radical reformers.

Contracting out is actively being promoted by a coalition of radical reformers and modest reformers. The coalitions have had the muscle to keep the contracting out issue on the agenda for more than a decade— despite poor records of concrete contracting out initiatives and cases.

The promoting coalitions have launched a number of initia
the period designed to keep contracting out on the agenda a
local governments and central government reflect upon the
debate becomes unpredictable in some respects because emp
continue to be discussed and debated. These cases are usually ̲controver-
sies or scandals—like in Farum, in the case of ISS and Sweden and ISS and
Aalborg. Seldom are favorable contracting out experiences reported. The
two promoting coalitions compensate for this by publishing reports full of
technical information on how to improve the contracting out process.
Some of these reports make the headlines, and others are drawn into the
professional discussion.

The professional discussion is what has been driving the contracting
out discussion. Most of the professional discussion takes place not in the
media, but in various kinds of professional forums that are set up to discuss and promote contracting out. The brokers do most of their work in
professional forums. This finding fits well with the ACF, which states that
technical information is debated in professional forums. We have not
detected a decline in these forums, but rather a continuation. These
forums include:

- Ministerial conferences and launch events
- Workshops, seminars, and conferences arranged by public sector
  bodies
- Workshops, seminars, and conferences arranged by private compa-
  nies and consultants
- Workshops, seminars, and conferences arranged by trade union
  organizations
- Think tank reports and launch events
- Electronic forums such as the Contracting Portal

The reports that have made technical information available include:

- Reports from the Ministry of Finance (responsible for policy for con-
  tracting out)
- Reports from the National Association of Local Governments
- Consultant reports ordered by various ministries that look into vari-
  ous issues related to contracting out
- Reports from interest groups and consultants not ordered by min-
  istries or local governments
- Reports from international organizations (OECD)

Professional learning takes place in the professional forums, and this
type of learning spills over into political discussions. An example is the
discovery that the factor that held most local governments back was that

they thought the writing and preparation of the contract was overwhelmingly difficult and caused an excessive workload. The brokers and the modest reformers went into action. A number of consultancy reports, including reports from the Ministry of Industry and Commerce and the Danish National Association of Local Governments, have been issued. A number of conferences and seminars have been held on the subject. A new Internet portal has been introduced that should help with guidance. When this technical information on how to write a contract is provided, the promoters of contracting out will have won over more skeptics. Each problem related to the introduction of contracting out is addressed in a technical fashion, and technical information is produced to address the problem. The question is whether technical information will be sufficient to solve what many people still regard as a highly sensitive and even ideological issue.

RELATIONSHIP TO U.S. EXPERIENCE

In the United States, contracting out has been a hotly debated topic also. Donahue (1989) noted how contracting out attracted both proponents and opponents. Writing in 2000, Donahue stated that even though the debate about contracting out was perhaps not so intense as before, there were still a lot of contracting out policies at the local level that might generate debate and discussion. Reactions to the work of Savas (2000) in book reviews have noted how contracting out is not a neutral issue for many people. Some think tanks continue to put forward favorable views of contracting out. U. S. unions continue to oppose many contracting out policies around the country. Although there has been a search for improved processes (see Cohen 2001), and renewed scholarly insight into the requirements of contract managers (see Brown and Potoski 2003), there is still fierce debate as to how much is achieved by contracting out. It would be fair to say that coalitions for and against it exist in the United States and that these advocacy coalitions continue to battle it out. Meanwhile, the "broker industry" has grown, and scholarly evidence now available from government offices, like General Audit Office reports and International City/Council Management Association (ICMA) reports, helps bring actors closer together on a basis of sheer facts. In manifold professional forums, technical information is made available and debated.

The findings of this chapter may be of interest to the U.S. experience as well. The findings suggest that one should look more closely at the existing advocacy coalitions in the United States. Is it possible to find the same variations that have been identified for the Scandinavian (Danish) experience, as we have reported on? Are there improvements in the technical information available, and does technical information make a difference? Is anybody paying attention to what the scholarly evidence is showing?

Third, are there indications that the coalitions are learning from experience or nearing each other's views?

CONCLUDING REMARKS

This chapter examines policy learning and change in contracting out, using evidence from Denmark in the period 1995–2000. It argues that the advocacy coalition framework was best suited to understand the complex processes that have driven the contracting out policy debate. Through the recording of 2,707 attitudes from 633 different actors, the chapter shows whether and how policy learning has taken place on this important topic.

The analysis makes three points. First, contracting out has been on the policy agenda on a consistent basis. The intensity of the policy debate has been kept level throughout the five-year period. Second, the pro–contracting out coalition has issued the most reports and has also consistently kept reports coming; there has not been a "dry spell" in the policy debate on contracting out. Third, policy learning has not taken place in an impressive way. There has not been a convergence of attitudes toward contracting out. The anti–contracting out coalition, or parts of it, has moved slightly toward a more positive attitude toward contracting out. Still a huge controversy surrounding contracting out remains. Technical information and public and professional discussion have not changed attitudes toward contracting out overall. Contracting out is still viewed as an ideological issue, more than a pragmatic administrative and managerial tool to be implemented.

What kind of challenges does this interpretation raise for the future policy debate on contracting out? One strategy could be to further strengthen the technical information and to reorganize some of the professional forums in which contracting out policy is discussed. Another option could be to focus more on "best practices," because the "bad practices" have tended to dominate media discussions, resulting in a bad image for contracting out on the policy scene.

5

Contractual Governance in the United States and Scandinavia

INTRODUCTION

This chapter provides an overview of developments in contracting, with special emphasis on the comparison between the United States and Scandinavia. First, we examine the overall trend toward contracting in the public sector. We divide the period from 1980 to 2001 into three distinct phases, and we track the development of the three main institutional forms—internal contracts, contracting out, and public-private partnerships. We compare the process and the organization of contracting in the United States and Scandinavia for the reasons outlined in chapter 1.

The material on contracting in the public sector—on which this literature review is based—comes from various sources: official government reports; reports by international organizations, such as the OECD in Paris; scholarly work by academics; and practitioners' reports and best-practice guidelines. A number of mainly scholarly works now aim to give an overview of the debate on contracting. Among the more recent contributions are Fortin and van Hassel's (2000) edited volume, *Contracting in the New Public Management*; Savas's (2000) updated book, *Privatization and Public-Private Partnerships*; Lane's (2000) theoretical introduction and statement on contracting theory for the public sector, *New Public Management*; and Johnson and Walzer's (2000) work on the United States, *Local*

Government Innovation. The now almost classic works of Kettl (1993) and Walsh (1995) are worth reading for their clarity and originality.

TRENDS IN CONTRACTUAL GOVERNANCE

Contracting has been on the political agenda in OECD countries since the early 1980s. Contracting has of course been a tool for governments all over the world for centuries, as most commentators are quick to point out (examples of historical contracting relationships include the Spanish queen's contract with Columbus, who then set out to discover America). According to the popular shorthand version, the "new contracting" originated somewhere in the late 1970s and caught on in the 1980s. Privatization "guru" Savas (2000) takes some credit for promoting contracting, although he does attribute the introduction of the word "privatization" to another management expert, Peter Drucker, back in the 1960s. Contracting got a boost in the Thatcher and Reagan era in the Britain and the United States when both leaders pushed for market-type solutions to public policy problems. New Zealand was another country that – under a Labour government—caught the gist of the contracting agenda and then set out to create a revolution in public management systems (Boston et al. 1996; Boston 1999). These developments happened almost simultaneously in the 1980s, and the experience of these governments soon influenced not only the OECD and other international organizations but also the rest of the world's governments in the quest for creating better public service for less money.

In this section we develop a more refined picture of the development of contracting. We divide its development into three phases: the ideology phase, the experimentation phase, and the pragmatic phase and then speculate on a fourth phase: the contemplation phase. In the following section, we explore the development of the three institutional forms— internal contracting, contracting out, and public-private partnerships.

The Ideology Phase

In the *ideology phase,* the first phase that contractual governance has gone through, the focus is on markets and market-type mechanisms for public governance. The word "privatization" was widely used; "contracting" was less often used in official parlance. The essential message was that markets would solve the public sector's ills. Contracts were a part of what Kettl (1993) calls "the competition prescription," but contracts were not heralded in themselves. The competition prescription was followed most visibly by Thatcher in Britain and Reagan in the United States. But as radical as these leaders were, the most wide-reaching effort to marketize and contractualize came not from Britain and the United States, but from New Zealand. And New Zealand had—as mentioned earlier—a Labour government.

The New Zealand model of public management has rightly attracted a lot of attention. It has been examined in great detail by a number of researchers (Boston et al. 1996; Boston 1999; Scott 1996; Pallot 1999). As a number of observers have stressed, it is important to note the background and context in which the public management reforms took place. Pallot (1999) distinguished among three phases of development in New Zealand: the management phase, the market phase, and the strategic phase. New Zealand first embarked on reform because of the poor standing of the economy and a rundown public sector. In many New Zealand observers' opinion, New Zealand had to do *something* to put the country right. There was no overall plan to begin with, although the reforms soon gained a consistent outlook because of heavy Treasury input. The Treasury input in New Zealand at the time was strongly influenced by the thinking of the new "economics of organization" school mentioned in chapter 2. These economists were able to—and were given room to—develop strategic plans to marketize and to contract out services.

Contracting was on top of the agenda in the marketization phase that had its heyday in New Zealand in the late 1980s. According to Boston (1999, 6), there was an "extensive use of 'contractualist' devices to govern the relationship between agents and principals within the public sector as well as between public and private organizations." Boston adds that specific contracts were manifold: "The most significant of these devices [contracts] are the annual performance agreements between ministers and departmental chief executives, the annual purchase agreements between ministers and departments, and the annual purchase (or funding) agreements between those agencies purchasing and those providing services (e.g. health care). Various other documents of a quasi-contractualist nature include statement of corporate intent, statements of intent, statements of objectives, and charters." In New Zealand, around 20,000 people worked for local government in 2000, and 15,000 people worked for organizations with contracts for providing public service.

The question for many people around the world has been: How does the New Zealand system work in practice? Again, there are a number of critiques of and discussions about this, although New Zealand has not had a tradition of extensive evaluations (save a few high-profile evaluations, like Schick's analysis from 1996). Boston (1999, 8–12) lines up the evidence so far. He states that there has been "significant gains in many areas" and notes the greater productivity of public sector organizations and improved budgetary control. He also notes how accountability has improved and how much more information on public services is available. Devolution of responsibility has caused the usual shortcomings of devolution (loss of central expertise, overlap, etc.), while government departments have competed for staff.

Boston also mentions accusations of fraud and bribery, although he adds that it is "impossible to determine" if the unethical behavior was caused by the introduction of contractual governance. Another incident—mentioned in most articles on New Zealand's reform efforts—is the Cave Creek disaster in 1995, where a viewing platform collapsed, killing fourteen youngsters. It was afterward found that the responsible public safety organization had failed its task.

Summing up, the ideology phase was concerned with introducing the "contract idea," and nowhere was it carried out with the same vigor as in New Zealand (although neighboring country Australia soon followed after). The ideology was more of a market-oriented ideology (later to be included in the New Public Management [NPM] term) than a party-political ideology dominated by the New Right (although both Thatcher and Reagan rode the bandwagon at an early stage).

The Experimentation Phase

The *experimentation phase* allowed a wide variety of new practices of contractual management to come forward. Initially, contracting in most places meant contracting out. In the experimentation phase, internal contract came on to the agenda. New Zealand was one of the first countries to add it, as we have just discussed. Britain experimented with performance agreements that covered the so-called Next Steps agencies, which were agencies that had contracts with a government department (James 1995). The experiment was taken up in a number of countries. Denmark, for example, experimented with so-called contract agencies (Greve 2000). Contract agencies in Denmark were first introduced in 1992 by the then Conservative-led government, but the experiment was carried on by the following Social Democratic–led government.

Internal contracts were introduced on a number of levels in the public sector. It spread from being merely agency contracts to personalized performance contracts, section contracts (covering whole sections in a department), and institutional contracts with government institutions other than agencies.

In the experimentation phase, the governments' strategy seems to have been: "Let's see how much public sector activity we can put on contracts." And so the hunt went on for new service areas, new organizations, and new subsections of organizations to put on contract. In Denmark, the number of contract agencies went from 9 in 1993 to over 100 agencies in 2000. In New Zealand, as we have seen, ministers' relationships to chief executive officers in their department became targets for contractualization.

Public-private partnerships also occurred as possible alternatives to contracting out. The partnership agenda has been promoted from an academic point of view (Savas 2000), from a government point of view (Danish Ministry of Industry and Business 1998), and from think tanks in Britain (IPPR 2001). Everyone seems to agree that public-private partnerships have something going for them and that experimenting with various forms of public-private partnerships is a good idea.

Both internal contracting and public-private partnerships can to some extent be viewed as ways to go beyond the more rigid privatization/contracting out debate. Both internal contracts and public-private partnerships offer refreshing views on how the public sector and the private sector should relate to each other. Certainly, the semantic difference between public-private partnerships and contracting out appears to make a lot of difference.

The Pragmatic Phase

The *pragmatic phase* is the name for the developments when governments, private sector companies, and nonprofit organizations decide to "get down to business." In the pragmatic phase, the words "cooperation" and "coordination" are on decision makers' and observers' lips. In the words of a senior person from the British Prime Minister's office, "What matters is what works" (spoken on the launch of the Building Better Partnerships report, June 2001, in London). The Blair government has made it clear that it wants to—in its own words—"modernize" the British public sector and that by so doing, it won't let ideological or traditional barriers stand in its way. Although this may sound like spin-doctors' outpouring of words, the need to be pragmatic about the public-private relationship is heard in many countries in the OECD world. The OECD itself has also called for a more "holistic" approach to management and governance (Wolf 2000). All governments seem to echo this notion of "what matters is what works."

The Contemplative Phase

The *contemplative phase* is a fourth phase we might add, drawing on inspiration from the New Zealand experience. The word is, from government and observers in New Zealand alike, that reforms have simply gone on too long and that there is a need to contemplate the results that reforms have brought. New Zealanders find many critical incidents in their pursuit of public management reform, including the contracting agenda. After noting the usual criticisms aimed at contractualist governance, such as high transaction costs, Boston (1999; 10–12) notes three "drawbacks" in using internal contracts in this case:

1. Contracts do not solve "fundamental tensions" in public management (Boston mentions resource allocation as an example).
2. "Contracts do not necessarily enhance political and managerial
   accountability." Boston notes that problems continue to exist with
   accountability and that responsibility is not clear. Furthermore, contracts can "complicate, rather than simplify" existing accountability
   mechanisms.
3. Not every aspect of human action can be contractualized. Here,
   Boston may be thinking of Durkheim's words that "not everything
   in a contract is contractual." Boston notes that "much rests, in other
   words, on generally agreed conventions, values and norms."

Boston's view of the New Zealand reforms with contractual governance
echoes that of other observers around the globe. Wolf (2000) hints that
there will be a wider agenda than just the New Public Management
agenda of the 1990s for the time to come, a point already made by various
academic critics of NPM for years.

EXPERIENCE IN THE UNITED STATES AND
SCANDINAVIA WITH CONTRACTUAL
GOVERNANCE

In this section, we first identify the services provided through contracting and the volume of contracting. Second, we look at the process of
contracting. Third, we examine the organization of contracting. To
begin, we should recapture the differences between the United States
and Scandinavia (se also chapter 1). The United States has a federal system of government, while Scandinavia has unitary systems of government, although Sweden, Denmark, and Norway also have very independent local governments.

Scope and Scale of Services Provided through Contracts

Contracting has been on the agenda for state and local government in
both the United States and Scandinavia at least since the 1980s. Kettl
(1993) notes how public programs in the United States have been delivered through public-private partnerships since World War II. As Kettl
(157) states, "almost everything can be—and has been—contracted out."
He also points out, "almost everyone contracts out something" (158). It is
hard to find a state or a local government that has all its production of
public services in-house. Most state and local governments have some
service that they let private companies or nonprofit organizations provide. Kettl's (158) other point, that "everyone contracts out different

things," means that there is a great variety in the actual services that various governments contract out.

Savas (2000, 3) has a very broad definition of privatization as "relying more on the private institutions of society and less on government to satisfy people's needs. It is the act of reducing the role of government or increasing the role of the other institutions of society in producing goods and services and in owning property." In state governments in the United States, contracting out is defined as "competitive contracting for public service with the private (also nonprofit) sector where contract monitoring and oversight remains with the state" (Pfiffner 1997, 2). Savas (2000, 70–71) mentions the tasks that are eligible for contracting out: "Most of the tangible goods—supplies, equipment and facilities" and "at the local level: roads, schools, and government offices are generally constructed for governments by private builders under contractual arrangements." He also mentions how "municipal governments contract with private organizations for 'output' services delivered to the public such as refuse collection, ambulance service, streetlight maintenance, street paving and a wide variety of social services—the last mostly through nonprofit organizations." Finally, Savas mentions "input services," like clerical work. He adds various "unusual examples" such as part of the coin production of the U. S. Mint. In Table 4.2 in his book, Savas (2000, 72–73) lists two pages full of services that have been contracted out to private providers. Johnson and Waltzer (2000, 3) note in the introduction to their book how "contracting with private business to manage agencies that were formerly considered exclusively public responsibilities, such as airports, prisons, and schools, is now becoming a more common practice." They add, "It is even possible to find cities in which only a skeleton crew of public management employees exists with the vast majority of 'public services' provided through contractual arrangements" (3).

Contracting out occurs across the country. Often-mentioned municipalities that contract out are Indianapolis, Phoenix, Philadelphia, Dallas, and Cleveland (Pfiffner 1997, 11). Other reports mention New York, Charlotte, and San Diego County (ICMA 1999; Savas 2000; Johnson and Waltzer, 2000). The International City/Council Management Association is one of the most authoritative sources of information on contracting in cities and counties in the United States (ICMA 1999; Johnson and Waltzer 2000). Contracting out is defined here as "a binding agreement under which a local government pays a private firm or nonprofit organizations to provide a specific level and quality of service" (ICMA 1999, 1). The ICMA sent out a survey in 1997 to 4,952 local governments across the United States. The results were as follows. Around two-thirds had conducted feasibility studies of contracting out within the last five years. The tasks most likely to be contracted out are "service delivery for public works, transportation, and public utility services and for health and human services." Private for-profit organizations deliver public works services while nonprofit organizations deliver health and human services. Until recently there has not been much contracting activity for safety, parks, recreation, arts, and cultural programs (ICMA 1999, 5). The regions most interested in contracting out are found in the Pacific Coast and South Atlantic regions, according to the ICMA.

Why do cities and counties engage in contracting out? According to the ICMA survey, the reasons given are decreased costs, external fiscal pressure, changes in political climate, and proposals from potential vendors.

Are cities allowed to compete themselves? Yes, according to the ICMA survey, one-third of the cities and counties allow "in-house" bids to be prepared, although mainly among local governments with populations of 50,000 people and over.

What is the opposition to contracting out in the United States? The reason most cited by cities and counties is employee opposition, followed by restrictive labor contracts and agreements and too few private sector deliverers (ICMA 1999, 18).

Expectations of contracting out are high. In his "transmittal letter" as chair of a Commission on Privatization, Pfiffner (1997, v) wrote: "The report presents ambitious recommendations which if carried out, can be expected to alter our government's approach to operations. All participants within the Commission recognized that management of state government must evolve, and that embracing more private sector provision of service will help the system to operate more efficiently."

Public-private partnerships (PPPs) have risen in scope and scale during the 1990s (Savas 2000). PPPs in the narrow sense are understood as "infrastructure" development. Noting the "lack of conventional public funds," Savas (2000, 237) points out: "Increasingly, therefore, we see private groups financing, designing, building, operating, and even owning infrastructure via innovative public-private partnerships." The scope of PPPs is a variety of infrastructure such as airports, correctional facilities, harzardous waste facilities, hospitals, housing, mass transit, municipal buildings, pollution control devices, roads and bridges, solid-waste facilities, stadiums, street lights, telecommunications, wastewater systems, and water systems (Savas 2000, 238, Table 9.1). The advantages of PPPs are that they attract investment, minimize the cost of new infrastructure, and "raise capital for other desired projects by receiving an up-front payment for the infrastructure concession" (Savas 2000, 239). Savas gives an example from his hometown, New York City, and notes that "demand for infrastructure is huge," but he fails to give estimates on a nationwide basis.

Contracting has been on the agenda for slightly less time in Scandinavia than in the United States. Discussions on contracting out began in the early 1980s, but did not evolve for some years. There was a fierce resistance toward marketization and contractualization of the public sector in the

Scandinavian welfare states during the 1980s (Andersen, Greve, and Torfing 1996). In the early 1990s, a renewed interest in contracting began to evolve. The trade unions were strongly opposed to any idea of "privatization." Scandinavian governments did not wish to pick fights with the trade unions concerning this question. Policy moves were therefore limited during the 1980s.

Discussions on contracting started in Sweden (Bryntse 2000). Because of a severe economic crisis in Sweden in the early 1990s, the government examined all ideas for making budgetary cuts and creating effective public organizations. One of the means used was contracting out. Swedish local governments began to experiment with contracting out initiatives in cities like Malmo and Helsingborg. The cities attracted international companies, like Danish-based ISS, to deliver services. The cities tried to "construct markets for welfare services" by dividing cities into service delivery districts. The cities tried to keep some public production expertise by not contracting all services out, keeping part of the production themselves. The most recently evaluated Swedish experiment with contracting out is found in the capital of Stockholm (PLS Rambøll Management and Concours Cepro 2001). In short, the cities were experimenting with various contractual models once "the idea/ideological" phase was completed.

The Swedish example was not followed immediately in Denmark and Norway. A major reason was the sound economic base of the two countries in the early 1990s. Denmark was about to experience an economic boom in the 1990s, while Norway had long relied on its "oil money"; money coming from the North Sea oil and sold by the state company Statoil. There was less fiscal pressure for Denmark and Norway to begin with. However, the NPM trend was also influencing both Denmark and Norway, and through this, there came a growing interest in contracting.

Like in Sweden, both Denmark and Norway deliver most of the welfare service through local governments. In Denmark, the local governments that stand out from the crowd with regard to contracting out are Grested-Gilleleje, Farum, Horsholm, and Frederiksborg Amt. Moderate contracting out has been attempted in a number of local governments, including Copenhagen, Aaarhus, Odense, Ribe, and Aalborg. Norway has not had many local governments with contracting out experiences yet, but the city of Oslo stands out as pursuing an experiment with contracting out (Fromm and Torsøe 2000).

There have been a few nationwide surveys of contracting out in Scandinavia. The Danish National Association of Local Governments conducted a survey in 2000 among all Danish municipalities. The survey was sent to all 273 members of the association. The response rate was 87 percent. We use this survey as the basis for the following attempt to give an overview of the Danish developments. (Note: A survey on contracting at the central government level indicated non-movement in the number and areas of services contracting out [Statens Udliciteringsraad 2000].)

What kinds of services are contracted in Scandinavia? In Denmark, local governments have contracted out services in virtually all service areas. Among the technical services, road repair, solid waste disposal, water-waste systems, building maintenance, and snow removal are the services most likely to be contracted out. In the welfare services (directly influencing citizens), the services that are contracted out are cleaning, transport, food production, meals on wheels, and accounting and auditing. The welfare services of day care centers for children, schools, and social services are hardly contracted out at all.

During the period from 1994 to 1999, around 1,800 bid rounds were conducted. Seventy-one percent of the bids were bids conducted for the first time; 28 local governments were responsible for roughly half of the bids (45 percent) in Denmark.

How do local governments choose between bids? In most cases, local governments go for the cheapest bids possible. In 50 percent of the cases, local governments made savings on contracting out. The tasks likely to produce savings are cleaning, accounting and auditing, solid waste collection, park maintenance, road maintenance, and wastewater systems.

Why did local governments want to contract out in the first place? The reasons mentioned most by local governments were aspirations to deliver services "best and cheapest," to produce cost savings, to get a private provider to deliver the service, to increase focus on quality, to create and inspire efficiency developments in other areas of the organization, to provide more choice to the users/customers/citizens, and to give the user/customer/citizen the chance to "buy extra services."

How did local governments prepare in-house bids? The answer is that they did not prepare in-house bids, although Danish law entitles local governments to do so. Nine out of 10 local governments did not prepare in-house bids. Why did the local governments choose not to allow their own employees to compete? According to the survey, 30 percent did not even consider the possibility, around 25 percent wanted a private provider to begin with, and finally, some local governments had already contracted a service out for years and could not be bothered to train new personnel to prepare the bids.

Why was contracting opposed in some cases? The most frequent reply is that the contracting out process is too demanding on resources and capabilities. Most local governments therefore refrained from even beginning. The second most cited reason was political unwillingness, most likely from Social Democratic mayors. The third most cited reason was European Union directives and regulation. Other reasons cited were fear of loss of influence during the contracting process, not enough competition on the market, not enough personnel to make bids themselves, issues of employees, loss of expertise, and employees' attitudes.

What were the challenges confronting local governments? The primary challenge is to formulate objectives for service quality. The second most cited challenge is preparing procedures that secure the legality and the compliance of the contract. The third most cited challenge is EU directives. Other challenges mentioned are deciding on criteria for choice of provider, employee relations, and securing flexibility in relation to changed circumstances.

What have the results been in terms of cost savings? In Denmark, 45 percent of all services contracted out produced savings, and 55 percent did not produce savings. Most savings were accomplished in cleaning and accounting/auditing. IT and food production/meals on wheels did not produce savings.

What has the level of quality of services been after contracting out? On average, 7 percent say "reduced," 14 percent say "increased," and 79 percent neutral. The figures are broken down service by service. Auditing and cleaning are the service areas in which there has been a drop in service quality. Service quality has been strengthened in IT services and food production/meals on wheels. Most local governments report positive side effects such as increased focus on work procedures, resource management, and quality control.

Public-private partnerships are found in a number of different settings in Scandinavia. They come in the institutional forms of joint-venture companies, as development contracts between a public organization and a private company, as joint public and nonprofit partnerships, and as various infrastructure projects. Greve (2003) has discussed public-private partnerships as alternatives to contracting out in Scandinavia (see also Collin 1998). In various government reports from the Danish Ministry of Business and Industry to the Danish Ministry of Finance, there is an increasing interest in public-private partnerships. A few local governments have been experimenting with infrastructure projects—for example, the local government of Farum—but recently the experiments have been blocked by the Danish Ministry of the Interior.

Discussion and Summing Up

Reports from the United States and Scandinavia show some similarities and some differences. The similarities first: Roughly the same kinds of tasks are contracted out in the two countries. Transport and technical services, including solid waste disposal and cleaning, top the list. There is an exception with regard to health and human services, whereby the United States tends to rely on nonprofit organizations on contract while Scandinavia prefers in-house production. The second similarity is between the types of local governments that contract out. In the United States several nationally known local governments experiment, like Indianapolis, San Diego, and Denver. In Scandinavia, a selected handful of local governments also stand out: Stockholm, Malmo, Oslo, Grested-Gilleleje, and Farum. The profiles of these "daring" local governments look alike. The third similarity is that contracting is still evolving in local governments; new services are added, new reports are being published, and new procedures undertaken. The fourth similarity is that employee opposition must be taken care of in both the United States and Scandinavia. The fifth similarity is that the motives for contracting out are roughly the same: to provide the best quality for the lowest possible price. The sixth similarity is that cost savings have been produced, but they have not been set against other objectives in a consistent manner. The seventh similarity is that both the United States and Scandinavia experiment with PPPs as alternatives to contracting out, but they are not quite sure how to do it yet.

Then we look at the differences. The first difference is that U.S. local governments have been keen to supply in-house bids in competition with private providers. In Scandinavia, this was absent. The second difference is that the evidence on which local governments base their decision varies; many U.S. local governments favor "Commissions of Privatization" before they embark on contracting, while Danish local governments either have little information or rely on consultants or government advice through reports and seminars. The third difference is, then, that contracting seems more entrenched in the local governments that actually go ahead than their Scandinavian counterparts. Contracting is a more institutionalized feature of U.S. local govenments compared to Scandinavian local governments.

Using Guy Peters's (1998) advice that the researcher should look at the similarities instead of the obvious differences when comparing two cases, we can claim to have discovered a number of important similarities.

The Process of Contracting

In this section, we compare the process of contracting between the United States and Scandinavia, using the "Kettl model" (Kettl 1993) of going through various steps of the process by asking What to buy? Who decides what to buy? Whom to buy from? What has been bought? Omitted here is the "Why buy" question because that relates to the more general consideration of whether to "make or buy."

Various examples of "the perfect process" exist. Savas (2000, 175, Table 7.1) provides the following 12 steps:

1. Consider the idea.
2. Select the service.

3. Conduct a feasibility study.
4. Foster competition.
5. Request expression of interest or qualification.
6. Plan the employee transition.
7. Prepare bid specifications.
8. Initiate a PR campaign.
9. Engage in managed competition.
10. Conduct a fair bidding process.
11. Evaluate the bids and award the contract.
12. Monitor, evaluate, and enforce contract performance.

In the United States, the "what to buy" decision is largely a matter for the local council and the mayor. As many local governments will have set up a "Commission of Privatization" (or Contracting), they have been alerted to the fact that they have to come up with performance measures and performance criteria. "What to buy" is mainly concerned with the quality of the service. An important part is to leave some discretion to the provider. In Denver, Colorado, for example, local governments are encouraged to "define desired results and expectations of the contractor, but the manner in which the work is to be performed is left to the contractor's discretion" (Pfiffner 1997, 9). The initial Indianapolis experience made the objectives output- and outcome-based, so that local governments determine the acres of grass to be cut or the level of child care service by the private provider in exact quantifiable numbers.

Identifying the "internal participants" in deciding on "the feasibility of private sector service delivery," the ICMA (1999, 18–19) study found "the manager/CAO, department heads, elected officials and the chief finance/accounting officer (for local governments over 100,000 inhabitants." For local governments of less than 100,000, the CAO is the most important person. The CAO is assisted by the chief finance/accounting officer and department heads. Also included in the decision process can be the public attorney.

Identifying the "external participants," the ICMA (1999, 19) study found potential service providers, consultants, citizen advisory boards, and CAOs and managers from other local governments.

In Scandinavia there seems to be problems with finding out "what to buy." The major challenge mentioned in the Danish survey was that local governments did not know how to formulate proper and credible objectives. Management by objectives (or "goals") are a feature of current reforms in local government (Hansen, Ejersbo, and Rieper 2000). But they have still not been incorporated properly in the majority of public organizations. In central government, there is still debate about how many objectives and what kind of objectives should be formulated (Danish National Audit Office 1998). The Danish Ministry of Finance (1995) has long fought a battle to persuade public organizations that goals and objectives can be formulated for more services than usually thought. In Sweden this is a different matter, as Swedish cities like Helsingborg and Malmo have had a longer experience with setting targets and creating objectives. "Who decides" is a local council decision, but in effect in the hands of the local government public managers responsible for the service area.

Whom to buy from is a delicate matter. As Savas notes, there is a need to "foster competition"; and one of the key lessons from a "competition prescription" (Kettl 1993) is that there should be enough companies out there wanting to provide the requested service. As often noted, in many areas in government services "competition cannot occur or doesn't exist." In Colorado, the number of Personal Services Contracts expanded from 2,625 contracts in the financial year 1994 to 3,085 contracts in the financial year 1996 (Pfiffner 1997, 20). The city of Indianapolis used a two-stage strategy to find out whom to buy from. First, they examined whether a service was considered a part of the government's "core mission," by what was known as the "core services test." If a service is not considered "core," then Indianapolis performs a "yellow pages test" to see if there are private providers that can provide the requested service. The "yellow pages test" is mentioned in much of the U.S. literature on contracting. It means that if a provider in the yellow pages provides the service, contracting out should be tried.

In the United States, the providers consist of three subcategories: private companies, private nonprofit organizations, and employees who are producing competitive in-house bids. In fact, as many as a third of the bids came from public organizations that had pulled together to present a competitive bid. Earlier, we noticed how welfare services were often provided by nonprofits. Other services, like transport or road maintenance, were provided by for-profit private companies. There seems to be a division of labor between these organizations (mostly between profits and nonprofits while employees' own offers compete with both). In the literature, however, an ongoing debate concerns how much the nonprofit sector should commit itself to solve public problems or to provide public service.

Service providers vary in institutional form and size. An estimate from Colorado was that Colorado contracts with over 4,000 private entities for various kinds of public services. In the United States, one major difference is between for-profit providers and nonprofit providers. Both types of organizations can vary in relation to being "local" or "national"—or even "international." The market for prisons and correctional services is dominated by a few large and specialized companies, like Correctional Corporation. The market for human and personal services shows much more variety, with a number of nonprofit organizations.

In Scandinavia, the "whom to buy from" question seems more focused on private for-profit companies. Some of these for-profit companies dominate their market. In Denmark, the market for welfare services is dominated by two large companies, ISS and Group-4 Falck. ISS was for a long time a dominant force on the Danish market; recently the company merged with its biggest rival, Jydsk Rengøring, to become one big Danish-based company (but with an international outlook). The Falck company has long dominated the Danish market for ambulance services and firefighting. In the late 1990s, Falck merged the British-based company Group 4 into Group 4-Falck. This company also operates in Sweden and Norway, as well as in a number of other countries, including Germany. The market for hard services like road maintenance is dominated by a few companies, with the local government–owned Tarco as one dominant company. In the waste management industry, there is another dominant company. In few markets do we see a fierce competition between rival firms. Where there has been rivalry in the past, there are now mergers and consolidation among the key players.

In Sweden, the situation seems a bit better. Over 40 companies have been involved in providing welfare services in the capital city of Stockholm (PLS 2001). In Oslo, Norway, there is also evidence of a number of players, although the Danish-based ISS is also present.

Nonprofit organizations appear to have played a much smaller role in contracting out decisions in Scandinavia than in the United States. Nonprofits are typically not so tightly organized in Denmark as the private companies or, for that matter, their nonprofit cousins in the United States. Nonprofit organizations are also not very large, and they have typically been less inclined to enter into contracts with the public sector on large public service delivery missions. In the past ten years, the governments in Scandinavia have tried to upgrade the nonprofit sector and to make it play an active role. This effort is institutionalized in a number of ways, for example, through the Centers for Voluntary Work set up in the Scandinavian countries.

There has also been focus on "active social policy" (Plovsing 2000; Danish Ministry of Social Affairs 2000), where the focus is on partnership and co-governing mechanisms between the private nonprofit sector and the public sector. However, as Paul Light (2000) has recently noted on behalf of the U.S. experience, there seems to be a limit on how much nonprofit organizations can be streamlined before they start to lose their original identity and raison d'être.

In the United States, control in form of monitoring and supervision is often the responsibility of the operating department. The "post-implementation audit" is carried out by the city auditor. Broader accountability measures involve the city council as the body that officially awards the contracts and acts as the formal "purchaser" of a service. Phoenix, Arizona, is the city where this division of labor has been used (Pfiffner 1997, 114). According to Savas (2000, 207), "contracting requires monitoring and enforcement, that is, a systematic procedure to monitor the performance of the contractor, compare it to the standards in the contract, and enforce the contract terms." One problem is how close and rigid the control process should be. Savas (2000, 207) suggests there is a dilemma: "Close monitoring is recommended but can deteriorate into micromanagement; in contrast, loose monitoring can lead to poor quality of service." The ICMA (1999, 20) study found that "cost" is what local governments control the most (83.6%). The second issue is "compliance with delivery standards" (80.4%). The techniques local governments used were "analysis of data and records (71.4%), monitoring of citizen complaints (69.2%) and conducting field observations (65.5%)." Perhaps surprisingly, citizens surveys are not used that often (28.4 percent use them). In local governments with less than 100,000 inhabitants, monitoring citizens' complaints is the method mostly used. In contracting out arrangements, control of the contract becomes essential, and control can be become more visible in some local governments, it is argued: "With long-term and short-term contracts, public sector control is actually increased because service delivery is now wrapped into a contract with requirements and responsibilities that can be monitored and enforced. . . . The kind of control that is given up is the day-to-day administrative burdens, regulatory compliance duties and technical functions" (Herbst and Seader 2000, 117). This is echoed by Johnson and Waltzer (2000, 183) who note how "cities must institute effective strategies for monitoring contractor performance when privatizing services. Simply turning a service over to a private firm without oversight can result in lower-quality services and higher costs."

In the city of Charlotte, North Carolina, the city makes sure that all bids are evaluated by an Internal Audit Division, and the method the city of Charlotte uses has been approved by Coopers and Lybrand, the big accounting firm (Size 2000, 226). The city of Charlotte is of the opinion that its system of audit and evaluation can be copied by other cities, like the rest of the managing competition program (Sizer 2000, 227).

In Scandinavia, "what has been bought" also involves questions of control, audit, and accountability. Control is usually control of costs and compliance with delivery standards. Costs have been the key issue for reviewing contracting out in Scandinavia for the past decade. There are, however, signs that other factors, like service quality, employee satisfaction, and customer satisfaction, are becoming important. Systems of quality control have been developed in recent years. In a contract for an elderly home in Horsholm, Denmark, the company ISS developed a sophisticated quality control system with recurrent updates of employees' performance. In Grested-Gilleleje, elaborate quality service systems have also been set up. A favored tool in Danish contracting out has been to institutionalize dialogue meetings between the local government purchaser and the private sector provider. These meetings are a way to get rid of rumors and misgivings about service delivery practice and to tackle the problems by their roots. Audit of contracts is carried out by accounting firms that can be either public or private. Kommunernes Revision is a company in Denmark that almost had a monopoly on auditing in local governments. This monopoly has now been lifted with the introduction of new legislation that calls for value-for-money auditing in local governments (as has long been the practice in central governments). Accountability rests with the central political and managerial top officials in local governments. Political accountability is a matter for elected politicians and the mayor. Managerial accountability is a matter for the CAO in the local government. There has been a limited use of techniques like citizen surveys, although some companies have been experimenting with "user surveys" within their own company jurisdiction.

The control of the services contracted out in the capital city of Stockholm is described as a mix between the local government's control efforts and the private provider's own quality control program. The politicians felt a greater need to let the public managers control the private provider than normal within the public sector (PLS 2001, 25). The Stockholm purchasers also made additional demands in the contract period that the private purchasers agreed to follow up on. Similar procedures have been reported from the Danish local government of Grested-Gilleleje. Politicians became more alert to complaints by citizens in Stockholm when contracting out (PLS Consult 2001, 26). The possibilities for filing complaints by citizens have not been altered either, according to PLS (2001, 26). In Stockholm, both purchasers and providers were committed to quality and quality reassurance, according to the Swedish researcher Almquist (2001, 695), who has examined the Stockholm competition program.

However, a number of the quality criteria were pitched at a general level and not a checkable or measurable level; Almquist (2001) observes that "the quality criteria that appear in the tender documentation are for the most part discussed in general terms and are primarily oriented towards processes" (698). Similar to the Danish experience, Almquist discusses how the Stockholm public sector agencies were not prepared to think in terms of management by objectives: There was no developed quality and management control system, there was no habit of measuring quality, measurement of inputs (not outputs) was the traditional method used, and the organizations were not geared to change in terms of their organizational culture. Another problem was resistance by professional groups such as social workers. With no clear objectives to measure, the control process becomes ambushed.

Summing Up on Process Issues

What are the similarities and the differences between the United States and Scandinavia with regard to the process of contracting out?

The similarities are found in the "what to buy" and "who decides what to buy" categories. Roughly, the same kind of people are involved. As the local governments get bigger, more people and more offices are involved in the decision. The smaller the local government, the more the decision-making process is centered round the mayor and the CAO. There is a common practice of drawing on the expertise of consultants for providing the material. We found in the Scandinavian case that many local governments find the process of formulating objectives and preparing the bidding material difficult and full of obstacles to be overcome, especially if the bid has to be prepared through European Union rules.

There are differences in the "whom to buy from" decision. American local governments have a broader variety of service providers to choose from than their Scandinavian counterparts. Also, the American market seems to have specialized more, so that nonprofit organizations will typically be delivering welfare services. American local governments also pay attention to preparing their own bids through their employees. In Scandinavia, the contracting out process is aimed mainly at private sector company service providers. As figures from Denmark showed, the employee alternative is rarely considered.

There are both similarities and differences in the "what has been bought" part of the process. The examination involves control, audit, and accountability in both Scandinavia and the United States. More emphasis is placed on compliance with delivery standards in the United States than in Scandinavia, where management by objectives was not fully developed in the 1990s. The process seems to be better thought through in the United States than in Scandinavia, where there has been a tradition of looking at input control instead of output control. Scandinavia seems to have had more experiments with dialogue-based meetings. In both the United States and Scandinavia, there is a focus on quality and quality systems.

Supporting the process in both the United States and Scandinavia are a number of professional organizations, international organizations, consultancy firms, and think tanks. Their role is to help the process along and to provide information on contracting questions and challenges. The ICMA plays an important role in the United States with collecting and systemizing information on contracting out. The National Association of Local Governments in Denmark performs a similar function. A variety of think tanks provide information and knowledge, perhaps more so in the United States than in Scandinavia.

Consultancy firms play an important part in spreading information and best practices. They do so both in their capacity as direct consultants and also as producers of reports on practices on behalf of various parts of the government. Finally, the OECD, as in other areas of public policy, performs a function in assembling and digesting material on contracting out (see OECD [1997] for an example).

THE ORGANIZATION OF LOCAL GOVERNMENTS IN CONTRACTING

This section examines how local governments organize themselves when they contract for delivery of public services. First, we look at the structure of government: Is it a centralized model, where all the decisions are made in one place in the administration? Or is it a decentralized model, where the decision-making capacity has been devolved to line managers or other staff? Another possibility is that decision making is, in fact, put in the hands of external participants, such as the providers themselves or consultancy firms. Second, we look at the market structure: Is it a competitive market with many players? Or is it an oligopoly with a few combatants? Another possibility is that the provider has a monopoly of service delivery.

Structure of Local Government

In the United States, there is in many local governments a division of labor within a centralized system. In the case of Phoenix, Arizona, the following parts of the local government organization are active: the operating department, the law department, the materials management department, the city council (and its staff), and the city auditor (Pfiffner 1997, 14).

The operating department is usually where the action is taken on contracting; that is where key policy options are weighed and where the decision is prepared. A report from a case study in Tempe, Arizona, on contracting for vehicle towing showed that the Department of Management Services was responsible for the idea of dividing the city into two zones, with a competing firm in each zone. In the end, however, the contract for both zones was awarded to a single contractor, which the department then had to deal with (ICMA 1999, 58–59).

The case of Charlotte, North Carolina, shows how the structure can change when contracting is implemented (Sizer 2000, 214–216). After a "privatization task force" had done its work, the city of Charlotte set about to make organizational changes. Previous to contracting, Charlotte had 26 departments. Each department had its own focused task to concentrate on. Under the new contracting regime, the 26 departments were transformed into nine so-called Key Businesses. The businesses are aviation, fire, neighborhood development, planning, police, engineering and property management, solid waste services, transportation, and utilities. Close to the city manager himself was a leadership team, with the deputy city manager and the assistant city manager. There also was a Support Businesses division consisting of budget and evaluation, business support services, finance, and human resources. Each of the Key Businesses had to present a business plan on an annual basis. The business plans included the objectives and the financial implications of the proposals. The business plan also functioned as a control device: "The business plans are also the main reporting tool by which performance measurements for the Balanced Scorecard and the City Council priorities are identified, tracked and reported" (Sizer 2000, 215).

In addition to the "internal" reorganizations, the city of Charlotte also established a "Citizens' Privatization/Competition Advisory Committee." The role of the advisory committee was to "monitor the progress of implementing contracts for services, to recommend services to be considered for competition and privatization, and to advise on ways to improve current contracted services with service delivery problems" (Sizer 2000, 216). Written guidelines were also issued.

In addition to the specific organizational committees, different policy initiatives were also developed by the city to support the process. There was a policy for employees' placement. A competition plan outlined the strategy for contracting and competition over a five-year period. And a "Competition-Based Gainsharing Plan" rewarded employees if they won a contract or performed better than expected. According to Sizer (2000, 216), the gainsharing was spread out with one-half going to the employees and the other half remaining within the production unit.

In sum, the contracting initiatives in Charlotte cover activities on a number of issues, both organizational and policy issues. The program is wide-ranging, as Sizer explains: "Managed Competition in Charlotte is an umbrella term for the host of activities contained in the city's competitive bid program" (Sizer 2000, 217).

Charlotte is an example of a city that has followed some of Kettl's advice on how to become "a smart buyer." Kettl (1993, 208–210) advocated that local governments need a different kind of bureaucracy, which entails hiring, training, and rewarding frontline and mid-level bureaucrats; making politicians aware of contracting issues; toning down the political rhetoric; avoiding contracting for "core" governmental functions; and recognizing that market methods raise new issues for governance.

The other part of the structure issue is the structure of the marketplace. All researchers are in agreement that it is no good to replace a public monopoly with a private monopoly. Savas (2000, 123) explains: "Total dependence on a single supplier, whether a government agency or a private firm, is dangerous. Without choice and flexibility, the ultimate consumer of public services, the citizen, is subject to endless exploitation and victimization."

Competitive markets do not always exist. As Kettl (1993, 180) points out: "The much-praised self-discipline of the market exists only when competition can reward success and punish failures. If market imperfections hinder such self-discipline, problems ranging from conflict of interest to fraud can simmer." And furthermore: "The actual markets in which the federal government buys its goods and services are thus very different from the assumptions and arguments embodied in the competition prescription" (182).

The optimal factor, seen from a contracting point of view, is having a variety of competitors to choose from. That does not mean that they will all be chosen in the end. But from the government's point of view, a number of competitors is good to keep prices low and quality high. A few examples from the literature can be related to this point: In the city of Charlotte, the city's Equipment Management Division wanted to contract for vehicle maintenance for the city's fleet of 3,600 units. Two private for-profit companies plus the city's own employees bid for the contract. The employees of the Equipment Management Division ended up winning the bid, ahead of the two private companies. The Equipment Management Division had adopted a lot of private sector management techniques to improve its productivity, and it had the experience with service delivery (Sizer 2000, 233). The team that prepared the bid consisted of the division director, the vehicle maintenance manager, a mechanic, the division's business manager, and a consultant.

In Phoenix, Arizona, managed competition is seen as a method "to ensure that in-house costs are lower or at least competitive to market costs" (Pfiffner 1997, 14). Phoenix has used competitive bidding in 13 service areas such as ambulance service and refuse collection. The city of Phoenix had won 22 contracts in the mid-1990s, and the private sector won 34 contracts. The policy is to divide the city into zones that come up for competitive bidding.

If companies have been in the market a long time, they may not be so easy to deal with. A quote from Colorado's Department of Human Services illustrates this point: "Just because something is privatized does not mean you have all the flexibility in the world. It is not as flexible to privatize in real world terms as you might sometimes think" (Pfiffner 1997, 21)

Local governments can opt for a "mix" of services, so that some services are contracted out, some are kept in-house, and some are organized as partnerships. Putnam County in New York State is an example, as the county has "five cases of privatization, six cases of intermunicipal cooperation, six cases of reverse privatization, and two cases of government entrepreneurship" (Warner 2000, 100). With such a mix, local governments do not rely on only one or a handful of contractors.

Governments may make it clear that they favor only one winner in the end. The process can be competitive in itself, but the competition does not extend beyond the contract agreement. After the contract is awarded, only one firm is left to produce the service. In the next round, other bidders can approach the government again. An example is wastewater-contracting in Indianapolis, where the city initially had five bids to choose from; after a selection process, which included two semifinalists, Indianapolis finally awarded the contract to one company (Savas 2000, 179).

The partnership agreement is seen in many areas. Here, the government does not choose a monopoly, but chooses to create a partnership with one out of many organizations. The city of Bend, Oregon, contracted for domestic violence emergency service with the nonprofit community-based organization called the Central Oregon Battering and Rape Alliance (ICMA 1999, 75–76). Maricopa County, Arizona, contracted for hospital management service from a company called Quorum Health Resources (ICMA 1999, 73–74). Volusia County, Florida, contracted for environmental policy expertise with the Nature Conservancy (ICMA 1999, 61–62). Peoria, Illinois, entered a partnership agreement with the dominant firm in the area called Waste Management Inc., a nationwide company (ICMA 1999, 43–45).

In Scandinavia, the organization of the local government follows both the centralized model and the decentralized model. In the centralized model, the local government places its specific decision-making capacity in the CAO/city manager. A special task force connected to the CAO to deal with the question of contracting. The task force will prepare and help to implement the contracting process.

The centralized model in smaller local governments looks like this: In Grested-Gilleleje's organization, the mayor and the CAO are both heavily involved in the contracting program. The responsibility is then devolved to the section of social services, where delivery of elder service has been contracted out to three different companies. The social services section is aided by an internal consultant group that has prepared the material for contracting. The concrete decision of whether or not to provide a specific kind of service is devolved even further to "a visitator" who makes the concrete decisions. The budget section reviews the costs. The whole of the local government's activities are audited by an independent audit firm. The local government is controlled by the central government through the regional "Tilsynsraad."

The capital cities of the three Scandinavian countries illustrate how Scandinavia organizes its local governments when contracting for public services. In Copenhagen, Denmark, a special "bidding/contracting office" specializes in contracting out. Also involved is the budget office of the city. Finally, experts in the social and human services section of the local government are in charge of the specific contract negotiations. In Oslo, Norway, the model is characterized as "a moderate, centralized and politicised model" (Fromm and Torsøe 2000, 34). The "centralization" refers to the process of preparing internal bids. Internal bids are assembled and worked through in one centralized organization. Divisions between employees who prepare the local government's own bid and the people who are about to act as purchasers of public service must be watertight. The purchasing task in Oslo is, on the other hand, decentralized to different "district city councils." The three decentralized local city councils that are open for competition and competitive bidding make up their own minds about which companies they want as providers. Stockholm has had a competition and contracting policy since 1993 (PLS 2001, 8). The district city councils in Stockholm are responsible for purchasing public service. In the period from January 1, 1998, to July 2000, 56 bids were awarded, each for over 1 million Swedish Kroner; 34 of the bids were awarded for the first time. Each city district council has a contracting unit as part of the district city council administration. A group of politicians is also connected to the process. For each bidding process, the contracting unit creates a project-based group that handles the concrete bidding proposals. For elder services, an advisory group of elder councils/handicapped people's council helps with the process (see PLS 2001, 14–18, for a detailed account of the organization and process in Stockholm).

Furthermore, two or more district city councils in Stockholm can combine their forces and enter into "framework agreements" with a number of larger private providers. The district councils can coordinate their purchases from the providers this way. District city councils thrive in Oslo and Stockholm, but were abandoned in Copenhagen by a city referendum.

What is the competition like in Scandinavia? The markets are characterized by some competition. In Denmark's local governments, there are usually from two to four competitors to choose from in the case of human and health services. In Grested-Gilleleje, three companies were chosen to provide service in three different districts for elder care (later, two of the companies merged into one on a national basis). For some services like ambulance driving and cleaning, the competition is not so great, as a few large companies (ISS and Falck) dominate the markets. In Denmark, there is a worry that there are too few competitors and that the situation is nearing monopoly conditions in some markets, as in cleaning or waste management. In Oslo, both private and public organizations have bid on the delivery of social services (Fromm and Torsøe 2000).

In Stockholm, a number of bids have gone down in the late 1990s. For 7 out of 10 tenders, there were 4 or more bids per round. In 60 percent of the tender processes in Stockholm, the competition was judged "good" by the district city councils. In the period from 1998 to 2000, 41 companies were providing elder and handicapped public services in Stockholm (PLS 2001, 14).

We see three different profiles within the Scandinavian case, if we judge by the capitals. The Copenhagen version is a relatively centralized purchasing model with only a small number of competing firms on the market and with no tradition for making employee bids. The Oslo version is a more sophisticated "managed competition-model," where the purchasing model is decentralized with a role for district city councils and where there is competition between private companies and employees' own bids (although they are separated by districts and not in direct competition with each other). The Stockholm version is a decentralized purchasing model with a role for district city councils, where there is adequate competition, but mainly among private sector companies. Summing up, Denmark is here "lagging behind," while Sweden is "ahead," but Norway is producing the most "sophisticated" model, involving both the public sector and the private sector in the competition.

The partnership model is not tested in earnest in the Scandinavian context for human and social services. There are some agreements that assemble partnership agreements, like a child care facility run by a private company in dialogue with the local government, but nothing on a big scale.

Discussion and Summing Up of Organization Issues

We can compare the similarities and differences between the United States and Scandinavia in organizing for contractual governance. The similarities first: There is a recognized need in both U.S. local governments and Scandinavian local governments to reorganize the local government once the process of contracting is decided. This becomes more important the more services are contracted out. This reorganization can involve (1) dividing responsibility between existing departments, (2) creating task forces or project groups, or (3) establishing purpose-built "contracting units." There is also a recognized need in both the United States and Scandinavia to try to "manage competition" and especially to "manage markets." Both the U.S. and Scandinavian local governments acknowledge the need to have a number of competitors to choose from.

The differences: There appears to be some variation as to how much the local governments decentralize their decision-making capacities. This, however, may vary within each country as much as between countries. The capital cities of Stockholm and Oslo have decentralized responsibility for service delivery to district city councils that takes over responsibility for contracting for public services. One American case divided the city's services up into new "business areas"; this more radical approach has not been seen in Scandinavia, where the emphasis still is on the social services section, the transport section, and the like within the local government. Another noticeable difference is that American local governments seem more keen to create partnerships with private companies or nonprofit organizations—despite the rhetoric of competition and advice from the research community. Judging from the available evidence, American local governments are more hooked on partnerships than their Scandinavian counterparts.

CONCLUDING REMARKS

In this chapter, we compare the theory and practice of contractual governance in the United States and Scandinavia. Surveying the contracting agenda in the OECD world, we notice the development of four phases; the ideological phase, the experimentation phase, the pragmatic phase, and the contemplative phase. We then compare the scope and the scale of contracting in the United States and Scandinavia. Following that, the process of contracting is examined, focusing on the Kettl model of "what to buy," "who decides what to buy," "whom to buy from," and "what has been bought" with the emphasis on a comparison between the United States and Scandinavia. We then discuss the organization issues connected to the contracting process in the United States and Scandinavia. Our concluding remarks concentrate on a few observed commonalities between the United States and Scandinavia.

The scope and scale of contracting is still developing—and has been developing throughout the last decade. There is no sign that we are at "the end of the road." In looking at the prospects for contracting, Donahue (2000, 161) observed for the U.S. case, "The odds are long that the next several years will see expanded outsourcing of federal defence functions, limited action for other federal agencies, a mosaic of experimentation in the localities and states, and hotly controversial but mostly marginal initiatives in education privatization." Apart from the mention of the military, the same characterization could be applied to Scandinavia. Certainly, there is a "mosaic of experimentation" going on. The scope for services to be contracted out is still broad. The scale of how much contracting could fill in the public management country profile has not yet been exhausted.

The process of contracting shows some remarkable similarities. The local governments that choose the contracting path are likely to commit themselves to the process. The kind of people who make the decisions are roughly similar in the United States and Scandinavia, both involving mayors and CAOs as the key principals. The "whom to buy from" part of the process involves scanning the market and preparing the market for competition, as well as making sure that a monopoly situation will not ensue. There is a difference in choice of providers. The Americans seem to have a broader variety of organizations to choose from—for-profit companies, nonprofit organizations, and employees' own bid—than do the Scandinavian local governments. The "what has been bought" part of the process involves different kinds of evaluative methods and is bound to involve control, audit, and accountability issues. The Americans seem a bit more advanced in establishing objectives and delivery standards that can be subject to control and inspection than the Scandinavians—but Scandinavian local governments are following suit. Citizen involvement is not so widespread as one might think, as the key means is still to monitor citizens' complaints. But advisory boards involving citizens group have been established in some cases.

The organization of contracting also showed a number of similarities. Most important is the fact that local governments do actually reorganize if they embark on a serious contracting strategy. The usual method is to create a special contracting unit or special project groups that are responsible for the contracting process. There can be some difference in organization according to the size of the local government, although smaller local governments—for example, in Denmark—have been known also to set up special contracting consultancy units. The markets are tolerably competitive in both the United States and Scandinavia, but competition in many markets is not fierce. More American than Scandinavian local governments seem to opt for partnership deals with private organizations.

6

Case Studies of Contractual Governance: Dane County, Wisconsin, and Odense, Denmark

INTRODUCTION

In this chapter we examine two case studies on contracting. Using the contracting process model developed in chapter 3, we ask why buy, what to buy, whom to buy from, and what has been bought. Each case study is preceded by a short introduction to the local government and the background for contracting in the local government.

Both local governments have something in common. They operate at the local level and are responsible for service production in their area. Both local governments operate within a political structure, with a political oversight body (the local government council) made up of elected politicians. Both local governments use contracts as one of their instruments for providing public services.

There are also differences between the two local governments. In the Dane County case, we examine the contracting of human services, whereas the Odense case concerns contracting of infrastructure tasks. Odense does not have a comprehensive practice of contracting out its human service production. Another difference is the amount of experience with contracting. Dane County has longer experience with contracting than does Odense local government.

Our main aim here is to compare contracting practice and contracting procedures. The type of service therefore matters less, although it can never be unimportant.

Data for the case studies were collected in Dane County, Wisconsin, and Odense Municipality, Denmark, in 2002. Semi-structured interviews were carried out with persons in both places.

BACKGROUND OF CONTRACTING

Dane County

The Dane County Department of Human Services has been contracting out services since the 1970s. The Department of Human Services has five major divisions: Badger Prairie Health Care Center; Adult Community Services; Children, Youth and Families; Public Health and Economic Assistance; and Works Services. In addition to that there are Administration, Fiscal, and Management Services units.

The Adult Community Services division has a mission to support older adults and individuals with disabilities so that they can remain in their community and to provide services that assist them in integrating their lives into the community. The Adult Community Service division provides services such as employment services, community residential services, treatment services, medical monitoring, in-home supports and day care services, case management and resources referral, transportation, and nutrition. Services are provided by Adult Community Services and 90 purchase of services (POS) agencies.

The legal statutes governing the department's work come from the Wisconsin statutes and the Dane County ordinances. Oversight is provided by the Human Services Board and the Health and Human Needs Committee. The Department of Human Services had a budget of $178.5 million for 2000 and a proposed budget of $187.5 million for 2001.

The Department of the Human Services buys services from 217 POS providers, which accounts for $98 million of the budget. Over 50 percent of the budget goes to external service providers.

The Department of Human Services faces decreasing or stagnant state and federal funding. It has to work better and cost less, like other public organizations in the United States. Among its challenges, the Department of Human Services mentions "the need to prioritize POS programs and put resources in critical areas." The department acknowledges that this will cause costs in other areas.

The Department of Human Services mission is to (1) develop strategies and information that result in basic, constructive social economic opportunities for citizens of Dane County, regardless of their individual characteristics; (2) provide basic support to citizens and families needing services in order to be self-sufficient, contributing members of the community; and (3) promote conditions under which citizens can be healthy.

The Municipality of Odense

Odense is the third largest city in Denmark with 287,000 citizens. It is located on the island of Funen, a small island in the center of Denmark. The local council has been dominated by the Social Democrats for the past 50 years. However, the traditional consensus among political parties within Danish local governments is also evident in Odense. In 1998 Odense changed its political structure toward a more traditional committee system. The change gave more power to committee members at the expense of the committee chairman.

The local council has 29 members and is organized with five standing committees. The committees are the Finance committee, the Children and youth committee, the Committee for technical services, the Committee for elderly care, and the Culture and social service committee. Each committee is supported by an administrative section.

Odense is normally not considered among the forerunners when it comes to contracting out services, but it has experimented with a number of different organizational forms at the administrative level, and with the use of management tools. It was one of the first municipalities to delegate economic and administrative powers to its service institutions and to implement user boards. User boards later became mandatory at all kindergartens, schools, and homes for the elderly.

As in most Danish municipalities, contracting is more advanced within the technical services than in any other of the municipal services. It is the area with the longest experience of contracting with private companies. The Technical Department is divided into five sections: public transportation, planning and environment, housing, parks and roads, and energy. Only the sections for public transportation and for parks and roads have organized themselves according to the purchaser–provider split model. The public transportation section has been subject to competition, but the contract was won by the public transportation section. As a consequence, the parks and roads section is the only section having an ongoing competition with private companies. The parks and roads section is in charge of tasks related to rivers and streams, recreational areas, parks, woods, graveyards, and roads. However, not all the services delivered by the parks and roads section are subject to competition.

The purchaser role is handled by the Construction and Operations office, and Park and Road Service has the provider role. Park and Road Service has a yearly average of 280 full-time employees.

WHY BUY?

In Dane County, contracting has been on the policy agenda for a long time. The local council prefers private providers. The decision to contract out a proportion of the human services is overtly political, as politicians in the county view the private sector as the "best" sector to provide as many public services as possible. The county board is not in favor of too many public employees, and keeping human services delivery at a distance is one way of keeping the number down. Dane County recently went through an overhaul when the county executive decided to take a look at the contracting system with the prospect of preparing the 2002 budget.

In Odense municipality, the municipal council decided on a tendering and contracting out policy back in 1993. The purpose of the policy was to make sure tasks were carried out at the highest quality at the lowest price. Furthermore, Odense wanted to increase efficiency through competition and market orientation. It was stated explicitly in the policy document that contracting out was not a purpose in itself.

WHAT TO BUY?

In Dane County, an announcement of a Request for Proposals (RFPs) is made. Bids are first scrutinized according to the price and the quality of the product. Then the bid is referred to the finance committee of the county. Then the bid is referred to the county board for a final decision.

The contract itself is divided into several parts. First is the boilerplate contract, which stipulates all the standard terms and conditions in the legal requirements. The second part of the contract (called "Schedule A") is about the specific service to be delivered. The third part of the contract (called "Schedule B") is about financial conditions. The fourth part of the contract (called "Schedule C") is about reporting requirements. The fifth part of the contract is about special features of the particular service that is not written down in the other parts of the contracts. The formal autonomy of the providers is recognized in the boilerplate contract, but in practice, the contract manager works closely with the providers.

The county can also decide not to take bids and simply negotiate a contract with a potential provider. This happens when services are urgently requested (an emergency situation) and the county already has knowledge of a potential provider.

As Dane County has contracted out services for more than 20 years, it has gained experience and knowledge in the field of contract management, and the position of the contract manager is well established. Contract managers oversee from 10 to 15 contracts each. Contract managers have often worked for contractors earlier in their career. A community services manager's responsibilities include contract management, which is defined as "planning, budgeting, monitoring and evaluating assigned purchase of service contracts" (Job Specification, Community Services Manager, Department of Human Services, 4/9/97).

The job specifications of the community service manager in 2002 included:

maintaining regular contact with assigned purchase-of-service contractors in regard to the authorization of client-specific services

managing service demand and service availability functions to ensure that older people and people with physical disabilities are appropriately served with an individualized treatment plan that promotes maximum independence in the least restrictive setting compatible with the needs of the clients

assessing the appropriateness of current purchaser of service contracts to meet client needs and recommending service expansion and/or reductions through annual review of proposals and issuance of purchase-of-service contracts

supervision of managerial and direct services staff including work assignment, planning, and direction.

The required standards of employment include five years of professional/managerial work experience in a relevant field and knowledge of administrative and budgetary management, as well as knowledge of the field of aging and physical disabilities.

A Human Services Task Force was created in 2001 with the brief of developing options for the county executive in the budget. The task force did not make any groundbreaking policy recommendations in the end, as opposition from the contractors proved substantial. The task force did succeed, however, in making the various organizations think about the pros and the cons of the current system of service delivery through third-party organizations.

There is clarity of the contractual governance system at the theoretical level and at the practical level. The county board oversees the contracting system and sets out policy. The Department of Human Services is in charge of the specific human services policy. The Adult Community Services division is responsible for the areas of Aging, Aging (long-term care), Developmental Disabilities, Mental Health, Physical Disabilities, and Jail Diversion. In the area of Development Disabilities, a staff of 1.5 managerial staff and 6 professional staff oversee 40 purchaser of services contracts worth US$61 million. Some 1,500 people are served through these contracts. Key programs and services are case management, residential services, vocational services, and day services transportation.

Odense municipality is governed by European Union legislation. In deciding what to buy, European municipalities must first of all observe a number of European Union rules demanding tendering of projects above a certain size (e.g., construction projects above US$5.9 million). In the policy document, Odense municipality listed several matters to be considered when deciding what to put up for contracting. If a task is contracted out, the municipality retains the overall responsibility. As a consequence, the contract must include a detailed description of the task and its desired quality. The policy document also points out that the contract must take into account the market situation, the possibility of comparing in-house production to private production, whether the entire task or only a small part is to be contracted out, the possibility of keeping in-house expertise if contracting in is needed or wanted at a later stage, transaction costs, the possibility of in-house bids, and the consequences for employment of the municipality's own employees.

The policy document gives the broad guidelines for contracting out in Odense. In one department—the Technical Department, contracting out and competition have been used on a large scale since 1994. Especially, the Parks and Roads section now has an extensive experience with contracting out and competition. The Parks and Roads section is organized according to a purchaser-provider split model. The office of Construction and Operation is responsible for the purchase of services. The tasks handled by Construction and Operation are divided into four types of services/tasks, where two involve competition and contracting out.

The Park and Road Service is the internal provider of services within the area of park and road services. The Park and Road Service can compete with private providers for the tasks subject to competition. For the remainder of the tasks, the Park and Road Service is guaranteed to be the provider.

Every year, the municipal council decides the fraction of the Construction and Operations budget that is to be subject to competition. Which tasks will be contracted out is the decision of the Construction and Operations office. According to the manager of the office, all tasks should be subject to competition at some point. The main purpose is to get the market price and an understanding of the situation in the market. The result of the competition may be to keep a task in-house, but knowing that the internal provider can deliver at a competitive price and quality.

Political considerations play only a minor role in selecting tasks to contract out. The municipal council wants tasks amounting to US$4.5 million (25 percent of the running budget) to be contracted out by the end of 2002.

WHOM TO BUY FROM?

In Dane County, the Department of Human Services contracts with a variety of providers. The providers are individuals, well-known nonprofit organizations like Lutheran Social Services (contract amount $3 million), for-profit companies like Dreamweavers Inc. (contract amount $2.5 million), and other local governments, like the City of Middleton (contract amount $33,000).

The interview data revealed that the relationship between the county and the providers has evolved steadily throughout more than 20 years of intensive contracting. The county knows the providers quite well: They know their financial capabilities, the specific nature of the work the providers are capable of, and which providers have good connections at the county board. The county recognizes the value of having nonprofit providers:

> We really work with a wide range of groups of agencies and organizations. One of the benefits with contracting is that each agency that we contract with, in addition to the services we buy from them, has connections in the community. Sometimes they can get more volunteers to work in their organizations and it helps them win the program. You get a little bit more value added because they are private not-for-profit. They may have connections that we do not have as government. (contract manager)

Some providers are heavily dependent on the county for contracts. Some of these providers may be small, one-person businesses.

At other times, the provider can be a nationwide service provider, and the local chapter of that service provider can extract most of its income from the county, too.

> One provider agency gathers over $10 million with contracts across the department. We have other agencies where the total contract is $2,000. This agency has over 25 or 30 different programs that we buy from them. Some of them are residential, some are case management, and some are therapy. There is a whole range of things that we buy from them. So it is a very complex system. They have a lot of influence on us, as do we on them because we provide 80%–90% of their budget. They are the biggest mental health, alcohol and drug abuse service provider in the county for public services. (contract manager)

This arrangement can bring out some tension when budgets are being cut:

> Today when we sat in a meeting with them, we felt some of the tension because the times we are in with finances must more uncertain. I think it's a healthy tension, but there is a tension. They [the provider agency] have a sense of what is quality, and they feel as a private organization that they should set the standards at a certain level for quality. (contract manager)

The providers have a substantial influence in both the community and the county. When a task force was set up to examine the state of human service delivery, the providers acted quickly to make sure that no human services program cuts would affect the providers. The providers can be hard to tackle politically:

> There is a big provider (a shelter workshop) which we put huge amount of money into. We (the county) wanted them (the providers) to get people out into the community and getting jobs. The only way we could do it was by saying, "We are taking a huge amount of money away from you unless you change the way you do business." There was a fury in the community because of all the families of the people who had actually been serviced in the workshop and truly believed that their children could only be served that way. So politically it is tough to take money away from contracts. (county board member)

The providers are always ready to fight the termination of a contract:

> Looking back over the years, we have had a lot of the same providers for a long time. Occasionally we have providers that are not providing a good service anymore. We have had some issues. There is a challenge of ending a contract. The providers have connections in the community and they will insert political influence, which we have to work within. It has been very educational! Almost every provider has an emergency plan they can call to the table and say: "Do not touch us." (contract manager)

In Odense municipality, the Construction and Operations office guarantees the internal provider, the Park and Road service, a minimum amount of business every year. The rest of the tasks handled by the Construction and Operations office are subject to competition. The bidding process is handled according to strict rules, and the procedures for opening the bids are heavily regulated and controlled.

The purchaser, the Construction and Operations office, has experienced only few difficulties in getting sufficient competition for all the tasks put up for contracting out. The manager estimates the average to be five bids for each contract. However, it is difficult to get more competition. One part of the problem is that there are too few companies in the market. Another part of the problem is the material delivered from the purchaser describing the scope and quality of the tasks. According to the manager of the Construction and Operations office, private companies find this documentation too detailed and voluminous for smaller companies to handle. The manager estimates the cost for a company to participate in the bidding process to be $7,500. Such costs may scare many companies away from participating in the bidding process.

The Construction and Operations office has not taken initiatives to create a bigger market or to foster competition. A few big companies dominate the market, but the manager sees no problem with monopolies. The manager feels that the Construction and Operations office has found a good mix between large and smaller contracts, attracting both large and small companies.

The internal provider wins about 55–60 percent of the tasks set up for competition. The manager of the internal provider section, Park and Road services, is quite satisfied with his record. He argues that he is not competing on a level playing field. As a part of the municipal organization he must pay attention to specific policies and agreements regulating work conditions and wages, which policies and agreements are much stricter than those private companies have to live by. However, being the internal provider also has some advantages. Despite the purchaser-provider split model applied in the department, some communication and collaboration take place between the two. The need to create a partnership between the two parties is also mentioned in official documents.

WHAT HAS BEEN BOUGHT?

In Dane County, performance measurement is well developed. In the boilerplate part of the contract, the terms of evaluation are stated clearly: "Provider will comply with county and other providers to define common data elements to be reported to county to assist in developing baseline data about program delivery, efficiency and effectiveness" (Schedule A of the boilerplate contract). There are clear specifications for consumer satisfaction measures, which take place on a biannual basis. The provider must survey its consumers, the county should approve the survey instruments, and people with no conflict of interest must administer the surveys. Strict guidelines govern how the results of the consumer surveys are presented to the county.

The reporting requirements are quite explicit in their demands on the provider. Quarterly reports must include information on waiting lists, quantity of services delivered, and progress or problems with achieving agreement goals and performance outcomes, and with overall provider operations. There are monthly client registration reports, and fiscal reports on a monthly basis (in a format chosen by the county). A financial and compliance audit must be carried out, with the provider submitting a copy of its annual audit to the county within 180 days of the end of the fiscal year. The provider must also agree to random audits by the county during the contract period. The reporting requirements are implemented in practice, and the contract managers feel they get information they can use in their work.

> Part of the contract requires that every month they submit to us both a service report and a financial report. Every month we get from them a list of all the people in the contracts that they are providing the right service. We get a list of all the clients, how many hours of service they plan to receive. So we

have a lot of ongoing information through the year from the agencies about their services. . . so we can use that information to follow up on the agencies and talk to them. You go and meet with them again. If they are having a problem or with their goals, or if they are not getting enough clients, we can talk about that and we can try and help within the agency. (contract manager)

When we asked the interim director of the department to give an overall assessment of the performance reporting, the director emphasized the value of the performance requirements, but also stressed that human services can be difficult to measure accurately:

I think the performance measurement is getting better. It is not optimal. Human services in general are real difficult to evaluate so the whole field naturally has been a challenge to us in some aspects. In some welfare services, performance measurement is easier. A person has a job, or not a job, they have to stay in a job, or they do not. It is trickier when you get into some of the softer human services programs like child welfare. Can you say with confidence that agencies have really helped prepare that family and child to be reintegrated? Can we be assured that abuse will not happen again? It is harder. I have watched the state of progress. I think we are better than we were, but have a way to go. Part of the problem is how you evaluate personal interaction with persons, which is what human services are. We have had to develop a significant infrastructure, mostly computerized, in order to accommodate the valid performance outcome structure. That took longer than we anticipated. (director of human services)

The county has ongoing discussions with the providers about what constitutes good care. The director meets regularly with a group of the bigger providers:

I meet with them regularly and our discussions have moved away from issues particularly to the services and to some of the broader issues. This group of providers was very instrumental about getting "The Living Wage Ordinance" passed in this community. . . . We are now working on benefit issues for employees. They are tremendous in lobbying the state legislature on human services budget issues. We provide them with the actual information when they are lobbying. (director of human services)

In Dane County, the performance data collection has been systematically taken care of. The county uses computerized systems. The contract managers evaluate the performance measurement indicators when they receive the reports from the providers. The county itself can also establish ways to collect data, like initiating a surprise audit of providers or turning up to inspect a program in person.

In Odense municipality, the contracting out policy does not mention very much about evaluation of the contracts or procedures to secure that the delivered service is in accordance with the contract. It has a sentence about the need to cancel the contract if the contract is not fulfilled.

The Construction and Operations office has clear procedures for controlling the providers. Usually the Construction and Operations office meets with the providers every 2–3 weeks. At those meetings, the provider reports back to the purchaser about tasks carried out, quality of tasks, and problems occurred during the period. The provider signs a document describing the quality of the services.

The system is based on mutual trust. The purchaser must rely on the quality systems of the provider. According to the manager of the Construction and Operations office, his office cannot conduct comprehensive quality control. The costs of even limited systematic control will cost more than the economic gain from contracting out. The Construction and Operations office makes spot controls, but these are very limited.

It is mandatory for providers to have internal quality control systems. The internal provider in Odense municipality has a control and quality system like the ones demanded from private outside providers. By signing a document, the employee guarantees that the service is carried out according to the guidelines and at the quality demanded. The document is used when the Construction and Operations office carries out its spot controls.

DISCUSSION

What are the similarities and the differences between the United States and Scandinavia with regard to the process of contracting out (see Table 6.1)?

Similarities are found in the "what to buy" category. Roughly the same kind of people are involved. As the local governments get bigger, more people and more offices are involved in the decision. The smaller the local government, the more the decision-making process is centered round the mayor and the CAO. There is a common practice of drawing on the expertise of consultants for providing the material that involves (1) dividing responsibility between existing departments, (2) creating task forces or project groups, or (3) establishing purpose-built "contracting units." In Scandinavia, many local governments find the process of formulating objectives and preparing the bidding material difficult and full of obstacles (especially if the bid has to be prepared in accordance with European Union rules).

There are differences in the "whom to buy from" decision. American local governments have a broader variety of service providers to choose from than their Scandinavian counterparts. Also, the American market seems to have specialized more, so that nonprofit organizations will typically deliver welfare services. American local governments also pay attention to

TABLE 6.1
Contracting Out in Dane County, Wisconsin, and Odense, Denmark

	Odense Municipality	Dane County
Why buy?	New policy	Integrated policy; scarce resources
What to buy?	Develop objectives; in the process of developing performance indicators	Develop objectives; clear performance indicators
Whom to buy from?	Small sample of potential providers	Large pool of available providers. Some have long-standing relationship with purchaser
What has been bought?	Report procedures in place, of both a formal and informal nature	Elaborate report procedure in place, of both a formal and informal nature (meetings)

preparing their own bids through their employees. In Scandinavia, the contracting out process is aimed mainly at private sector company service providers. Employee bids are not common, although legislation allows it.

There are both similarities and differences in the "what has been bought" part of the process. The examination involves control, audit, and accountability in both Scandinavia and the United States. More emphasis is placed on compliance with delivery standards in the United States than in Scandinavia, where management by objectives was not fully developed in the 1990s. The process seems to be better thought through in the United States than in Scandinavia, where there has been a tradition of looking at input control instead of output control. Scandinavia experiments with dialogue-based meetings, but an ongoing dialogue for accountability purposes is also a feature of the U.S. system, as witnessed by Dane County's relations with its providers in human and social services delivery. In both the United States and Scandinavia, there is a focus on quality and quality systems, although they are more elaborate in the United States.

SUMMARY

The process of contracting shows some remarkable similarities in the cases studied here. The local governments that choose the contracting path are likely to commit themselves to the process. The kinds of people who make the decisions are roughly similar in the United States and Scandinavia, both involving the mayor and the CAO as the key principals.

Most important is the fact that local governments do actually reorganize if they embark on a serious contracting strategy. The most frequently applied method is to create a special contracting unit or special project groups that are responsible for the contracting process. Organization may differ according to the size of the local government, although smaller local governments, as in Denmark, have been known also to set up special contracting consultancy units.

The "whom to buy from" part of the process involves scanning the market and preparing the market for competition, as well as making sure that no monopoly situation is created. There is a difference in choice of providers: Americans seem to have a broader variety of organizations to choose from— for-profit companies, nonprofit organizations, and employees' own bid— than do the Scandinavian local governments. The markets are tolerably competitive in both the United States and Scandinavia, but the competition in many markets is not fierce. More American than Scandinavian local governments seem to opt for partnership deals with private organizations.

The "what has been bought" part of the process involves different kinds of evaluative methods and is bound to involve control, audit, and accountability issues. The Americans seem a bit more advanced in establishing objectives and delivery standards that can be subject to control and inspection than are the Scandinavians, but Scandinavian local governments are following suit. Citizen involvement is not so widespread as one might wish, as the key means of finding out what has been bought is still to monitor citizens' complaints.

The policy implications of the comparative study are probably greater for Scandinavia than for the United States. The Scandinavian countries are currently moving toward a more market-based type of public service delivery system. Looking to the U.S. experience in grappling with questions of what to buy and whom to buy from and determining what has been bought can be helpful to Scandinavian policymakers and public managers. The Americans may learn from the "dialogue-based" model that characterizes some purchaser-provider relationships, at least at the evaluation stage, but extensive dialogue is also present in some of the U.S. examples of contractor-purchaser relationships. The advent of public-private partnerships is likely to support the dialogue-based model.

Theoretically, there is a need to further refine the "Kettl model" and to draw more variables into the framework. The work by Romzek and Johnston (2002) and their model of effective contract implementation and management serve as a strong inspiration in future efforts. One aspect to be explored further is the "contractual culture framework" that underlines the negotiations and governance aspirations of purchasers, providers, and customers. By comparing the U.S. and Scandinavian experience, we hope to shed light on the usefulness of this approach to the study of contractual governance and of contracts as reinvented institutions in the public sector.

7

Performance-Based Contracting in Local Government

INTRODUCTION

Much contracting takes place as contracting out, when a government buys goods and services from private providers through a contractual arrangement. What is new or relatively new, according to Behn and Kant (1999), is performance contracting. Performance contracting must "specify the type and level of performance that the vendor is to achieve" (Behn and Kant 1999, 471). Performance contracting is thus closely linked to performance measurement, which has been much discussed and analyzed in the literature on public management (DeBruijn 2002).

The model of performance measurement is relatively simple. The government specifies the performance criteria in the form of a desired output or outcome. The provider seeks to fulfill the performance criteria under time restraints and a limited amount of resources. The government then determines whether the performance measures are met through a check on performance indicators. The feedback to the government will reveal whether the performance measurements must be corrected if the cycle is to start all over again.

The idea of performance contracting has moved inside local government; we can use the term *internal contracting*. The idea of using a contract to regulate the relation between a principal and an agent is now used within local governments as internal contracting or performance contracting. Contracting as contracting out has been on the top of the public management agenda in Scandinavian local governments for some time.

When a government decides to use contracting within the government, it must find out what it is going to buy. In many governments, this has not necessarily been a natural task. Path dependencies and tradition have led governments to direct the production of goods and services in traditional ways. Performance measurement and performance contracting have changed that. Now governments want to know what they are buying and to specify the requirements in performance measures and performance contracts, even within the government. For many governments, performance contracting is a way of practicing how to buy goods and services from providers, even if the providers remain internal. Should the day come when a government wants to contract out the provision of public services, it will have the experience of finding out what to buy and specifying this in performance measures.

The biggest difference is that public purchasers will buy "inside" the public sector and will not choose from a range of private providers. Usually, the provider will be the sole "choice" for the purchaser in a monopoly situation. It is possible to try to develop "internal markets" (Taylor-Gooby 1998) for the provision of public services. This has been tried for a number of years in the British National Health Service. The internal market will not be a real marketplace because the price will not be determined only by the level of competition and many of the providers will not be allowed to go bankrupt, but a choice will be available among a number of "licensed" providers that are publicly owned. The monopoly situation leaves the purchaser in a principal-agent situation. The provider-as-agent may have more knowledge and have more discretion in operations than the purchaser-as-principal. Creating an internal market and managing and governing the market become tasks for the public purchaser of goods and services.

The evaluation of the internal contract is likely to be based on the quality of the performance measures set up in the beginning. Also, the organizational and governing capacity of the purchaser will play a role. The government must establish systems of control and evaluation to determine what has been bought. The interesting matter is if there are sanctions connected to the control and evaluation system.

The wider question with control and evaluation has more to do with public sector accountability than the control of performance measures in a narrower sense. Contracting has the potential to blur known lines of hierarchical responsibility because new organizational units will have managerial responsibility. Yet, contracting can also strengthen accountability, as the performance measures are easy to control and follow up, according to some proponents.

Performance measurement is usually said to have the following advantages: an increased focus on the objectives of an organization (instead of just production), a renewed cultural focus in a group on a common goal, an easier way to see how public resources are spent, and an opportunity to correct unwanted directions in an organization (DeBruijn 2002). Domberger (1998, 160–165) describes the advantages of performance contracts inside the public sector as (1) separation of purchaser and provider roles, (2) specifications, (3) competition (in the shape of internal markets), and (4) monitoring contractor performance.

Several disadvantages are connected to performance measurement: The organization may become too obsessed with specific goals and neglects innovation. Goals do not allow natural interest groups within the organization to function properly. Goals encourage a sometimes risk-averse culture in an organization. Performance measurements try to measure areas and services that may not be measurable. Performance measurement tends to focus on substantial outputs and outcomes while neglecting process variables (DeBruijn 2002). According to Domberger (1998), the disadvantages or difficulties of performance contracting are (1) the non-contractibility of quality, (2) ownership of physical assets (or "asset specific," in Williamson's term), and (3) public sector accountability. He also mentions the effect on employment, but that point seems more directed toward contracting out.

This chapter explores the use of performance contracting within local governments in Denmark. We ask two questions:

- What sets apart municipalities using internal performance contracting from other municipalities?
- What characterizes the process of internal performance contracting?

In answering the first question, we look at the importance of size, political leadership, and the prior use of managerial tools. The second question is addressed by using the framework introduced in chapter 3. We analyze the process by asking our four questions: Why buy? What to buy? Whom to buy from? What has been bought?

THE DATA

The following analyses are based on a survey of all Danish municipalities concerning the use of internal performance contracting. The survey was distributed by e-mail and was conducted in collaboration with the National Association of Local Governments in Denmark. The survey was sent to chief executive officers in every local government in Denmark. The survey took place in the fall of 2002. By November 2002 all the responses were collected; 158 out of 275 local governments answered the survey, a response rate of 61 percent, which can be considered satisfactory. An analysis of the local governments not included in the final data set showed no biases.

WHAT SETS APART MUNICIPALITIES USING INTERNAL PERFORMANCE CONTRACTING FROM OTHER MUNICIPALITIES?

The use of internal contracting by local governments may be accounted for by looking at several factors. We limit the analysis to include size, political ideology, and the prior use of managerial tools.

Size is an explanatory factor often used when analyzing different aspects of local governments. The size of the organization is expected to influence the likelihood of using internal contracting. As the size increases, the structure of the organization becomes more differentiated and complexity increases. In order to handle the differentiated and complex organization, more coordinating devices must be used. This means that we should expect sharper lines drawn between the operators who do the work and the managers who coordinate it (Mintzberg 1983, 124). We therefore expect large municipalities to use internal contracting more often than small ones.

Contracting is part of the new public management wave rolling across Scandinavian local governments. The many reform initiatives included under the heading of new public management are based on a liberal ideology, and in England and New Zealand they are supported by liberal and conservative governments (Lane 2000). It would be obvious to expect a local government with a conservative/liberal majority to be more supportive of internal contracting than social democratic–led local governments. However, Danish local governments are often characterized as pragmatic when it comes to political ideology, and political ideology is usually not expected to be of importance. Studies of contracting out in Danish local governments show that political ideology does not seem to have the expected influence on the use of contracting out (Pallesen 2002).

Within sociological institutional theory, administrative reforms are described as "organizational recipes" traveling among organizations (Røvik 1998). Organizations take in specific reforms and managerial tools in order to gain legitimacy. But reforms and managerial tools are like fashion—they are modern for only a relatively short time; in order for organizations to be modern and gain legitimacy, they must take in new reforms and managerial tools. Based on this argument, local governments that previously have used reforms and new managerial tools can also be expected to use internal contracting more often than those without a history of reforms.

In the survey, 41 percent of the local governments confirmed that they used performance contracting as a management and governing tool. However, the percentage might be higher than revealed here. First of all, many local governments who answered the question of contractual governance negatively were in the process of preparing for contracting. Second, the National Association of Local Governments is often contacted by local governments interested in knowledge about internal contracting. Overall, this leaves us with the picture that roughly half of Denmark's local governments are using performance contracting as a management and governing tool; most likely, the number will increase during the next year.

The use of internal contracting has increased tremendously over the past couple of years. As showed in Figure 7.1, a very limited number of local governments used contracting in the early and mid 1990s, while it has picked up speed since 2000. This development is supported by an increasing fiscal pressure on local governments over the past couple of years. When the government headed by Fogh Rasmussen took office in 2001, it was determined to keep its promise of "no more taxes." As a consequence, the Fogh Rasmussen office put severe pressure on local governments not to increase local taxes and even penalized local governments that raised their taxes. As a consequence, local governments had to control spending even more than usual and needed new systems and tools to control and manage decentralized service institutions.

Figure 7.1   Introduction of internal contracting, by year.

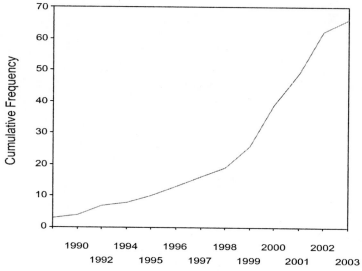

Year when internal contracting was introduced

We now turn to the question of what sets apart local governments using internal contracting from local governments not using internal contracting. First, our assumptions about the influence of size are supported by the data. As shown in Table 7.1, a very clear correlation exists between government size and the use of internal contracting. Larger local governments use internal contracting more often than smaller local governments ($p < 0.001$).

Political ideology cannot explain the use of contracting. As expected, we do not find any clear pattern of political ideology. There is practically no difference between municipalities headed by mayors from right-wing or left-wing parties.

To test the importance of the prior use of reforms and management tools, we draw on a survey conducted in 1997 in cooperation with the National Association of Local Government. The survey, sent out to all 275 municipalities, covered the use of different reform elements and management tools.

We use two types of measurements to cover the prior reform history. (Note: The measurement of reform history used here includes only a few elements. We are currently working to expand the measurement of reform history.) First, we look at the prior use of different management tools at service institutions (formulating overall objectives for the institution, measurements of quality, user surveys, evaluation, and service information). We find a significant relationship between the use of different management tools at a service institution and the use of internal contracting ($p < 0.005$). However, the relationship is not as expected (see Table 7.2).

It is apparently those municipalities not using internal contracting that use the different management tools at municipal service institutions. This finding may call for a rational explanation instead of the one inspired by the sociological new institutionalism presented earlier. Local governments already using a wide set of management tools directed toward service institutions have sufficient management tools and do not need to introduce contracting.

TABLE 7.1
The Relationship between the Size of the Local Government and the Use of Internal Contracting (in percentages)

	Size of municipality			
Using internal contracting	0–10,000 Population	10,001–15,000 Population	15,001–20,000 Population	Over 20,000 Population
Yes	29	40	56	71
No	71	60	44	29
Sum	100	100	100	100
N	76	37	16	28

TABLE 7.2
The Correlation between the Use of Management Tools and Internal Contracting (in percentages)

	Number of management tools at service institutions	
Using internal contracting	Two or less	Three or more
Yes	52	28
No	48	72
Sum	100	100
N	52	92

The second measurement used concerns the practice of formulating objectives concerning central service areas (management by objectives). The formulation of objectives can be seen as the first step toward internal contracting. Politicians and administrations get some practice in formulating objectives, but not in the same formalized way used in internal contracting. In Table 7.3 the results are displayed. No clear pattern is evident between the extent to which objectives have been formulated and the use of internal contracting.

To summarize, we found a significant correlation between the size of a government and use of internal contracting. This was expected. Looking at political ideology did not generate any explanation. The findings confirmed the limited importance of party ideology at the local level. The expectation that the prior history of reforms and use of managerial tools would influence the use of internal contracting did not get any support.

THE PROCESS OF INTERNAL PERFORMANCE CONTRACTING

To analyze the process of internal performance contracting, we use the internal factors in the framework introduced in chapter 3. In that framework, the following four questions are used to describe the process: Why buy? What to buy? Whom to buy from? What has been bought?

TABLE 7.3
The Correlation between Formulation of Objectives and Internal Contracting (in percentages)

	Formulation of objectives	
Using internal contracting	Objectives formulated at less than 8 service areas	Objectives formulated at 8 or more service areas
Yes	38	29
No	62	71
Sum	100	100
N	120	24

Why Buy?

We start by looking at the motives for introducing contracting within the government: "Why buy?" The different objectives behind the introduction of internal contracting can be summarized into four sets of motives. One set of motives is directed toward creating competition between different service institutions within local governments. A second set of motives concerns the future of local governments in terms of long-term savings and preparing for competition from private and nonprofit organizations. Third, the introduction of internal contracting can be linked to concerns about service and quality. It can be seen as a tool to make the system and level of service more transparent to politicians and users. In addition, it can direct the attention of the administration and service institutions toward developing the quality of services. A fourth set of motives is aimed at getting better steering and management of the service institutions, first by giving politicians better tools to control the level of service and second by making the connection between the level of resources and the level of service more visible. The relative importance of these sets of motives is reported in Table 7.4.

The desire to create competition among different sections within the local government is not the driving force when local governments use internal contracting. Nor is it concerns about how the local government handles future challenges economically or in terms of competition from external organizations. As will be shown later, the lack of importance given to the creation of competition as a sign of introduction of a "hard" contracting regime corresponds with the general attitude toward contracting within local governments.

The introduction of contracting within local governments is much more connected to concerns about the level of service and quality, on one hand, and about steering and management, on the other. The priority given to these two sets of motives must be seen in connection with the overall debate about the capacity of local governments to deliver service at a proper level and their ability to control their own budget and economic situation. Denmark is in the midst of a major change in local and regional

TABLE 7.4
Motives for Internal Contracting

Motives for contracting within the government	Index: 100 = very important; 0 = no importance
Competition	36
The future of local governments	52
Service and quality	79
Steering and management	80

government structure; how local governments perform their current tasks may be of importance when the future structure of local governments is to be determined.

What to Buy

The second question is "what to buy?" In answering, we start by looking at the different areas within local governments covering internal contracting. Second, we examine who are involved in the decision and whether local governments have made special organizational arrangements to handle questions related to quality levels, resources, and the like.

We find that contracts are used in all the major areas within local governments. They are used in areas with separate service institutions (schools, day care centers, homes for the elderly) and in relation to administrative sections within the town hall. As shown in Table 7.5, the technical area is the area mainly covered by internal contracts. About one-third of local governments are using contracting in relation to the technical area. That the technical area is the one covered in most local governments comes as no surprise. The technical area has a long history of contracting out and is as such no stranger to using contracts as a management tool. Between one-fourth and one-fifth of the local governments report using contracts within elder care, day care, and culture/leisure. The lowest percentage reported is found in social services. Again, familiarity may be the explanation. The social area has shown the most resistance toward other new management tools, and this general hesitation explains the modest spread of contracting within the social area.

Of the local governments using internal contracting, 20 percent use it across the board, covering all seven major areas within the local government. Of the local governments reporting using internal contracting, 27 percent are using it only within one area. The number of local governments using contracting in two to six areas is distributed fairly equally. This implies that the use of internal contracting is pragmatic and selective, not an "all or nothing" policy. The distribution of areas displayed in Table

TABLE 7.5
The Use of Internal Contracting by Area (in percentages)

Culture/leisure	21
Elder care	24
School	17
Social services	14
Administration	18
Technical	31
Day care	22

7.5 indicates that contracting is used selectively, taking local traditions into account.

The data show that in more than three-fourths of the local governments using contracting, the political level (council or committee) is one party to the contract. In the remaining local governments, it is left to the administration to sign the contract. This is not surprising, given that the political system is built on the assumption that politicians have standing to make decisions.

When asking who has influenced which areas are covered by internal contracts, the importance of the top management team and especially the CAO becomes evident. The mayor has some influence as well, while the city council and the committees only play a minor role. The lack of influence on the part of the committees is somewhat surprising. Formally, the committees have an important part in Danish local governments and could be expected to have an important role in influencing what areas are covered by contracts. The managers of the institutions potentially covered by contracts are reported to have more influence on the areas covered than the city council and committees. In all, which areas are to be covered by contracts seems to be decided among a small group of top managers and the mayor. The strong influence by the top management level confirms the general position of the management in Danish local governments (Klausen and Magnier 1998).

When using contracting, governments are advised to make a clear split between the purchaser and the provider (Lane 2000). For most local governments in Denmark, following this recommendation would require a major reorganization. However, the data from the survey show that Danish local governments for the most part keep their traditional form of organization. Almost half of the local governments using internal contracting have made no changes in their organizational structure. Another 25 percent have made a special purchaser section in the relevant departments. Of the remaining local governments, some are in the process of establishing a purchaser unit, some have placed the responsibility for purchasing in the top management team, and yet others have made special local arrangements.

Another aspect of organizing internal contracting concerns the contract itself. First we look at who are involved in describing the specifics and demands of the services/tasks put into the contract; second, we examine the content of the contract.

The description of service specifications and demands has a somewhat bottom-up approach. Whereas the decision to use internal contracting and the selection of areas to be covered by internal contracting are matters for the top political and managerial level, the political committees and leaders at each service institution have much more influence when it comes to describing service specifications and the demands to be put into the contract. As shown in Table 7.6, the leaders of the service institutions are

TABLE 7.6
Who Influences the Specifications and Demands Put into the Contract?

Actors influencing to a large extent	Percentage
City council	12
Mayor	10
Committee	36
CAO	34
Internal consultants	35
Leaders at the service institutions	58

reported to be the most influential, but the committee is also reported to have substantial influence.

As shown in Table 7.7, the contracts are oriented toward specifying objectives for quality, both overall and more specifically. It is also seen as a tool to improve the dialogue between the different levels of the local government organization. The most interesting finding is the lack of sanctions build into the contract. The lack of sanctions combined with the focus on dialogue point toward a more "soft" or relational type of contract. As discussed later, the soft approach to contracting seems to be an overall characteristic of internal contracting in Danish local governments.

Whom to Buy From?

The third question concerns whom to buy from. Here, there is not much to discuss, as no local governments have developed real internal markets. Yet the division of providers into narrower "profit centers" makes room for a soft approach to benchmarking between organizations. However, as pointed out earlier, the possibility of benchmarking different institutions within local governments does not seem to be a motive when using internal contracting. So far, internal contracting in local governments is internal in two ways. First, it is an activity taking place within a single local

TABLE 7.7
What Characterizes the Content of the Contract?

Content of contract, to a large extent	Percentage
Overall objectives related to the quality of the services	56
Specific objectives related to the quality of the services	45
Demands on the use of economic resources	33
Sanctions if objectives are not met	6
A setup for a formalized dialogue between the political level, the administration, and the service institutions	42
A setup to include demands from the political level during the period of the contract	28

government. Second, the contract between the council and a specific service institution (e.g., a school) is "living its own life" separate from contracts between the council and other service institutions within the same area.

What Has Been Bought?

From theories of evaluation, we know that evaluation is a difficult task. All too often, evaluation is either not carried out or has no consequences. The local governments using internal contracting seem to be aware of the difficulties—or part of them. Of the local governments using internal contracting, 90 percent report that systematic evaluation is carried out.

It is left to the service institutions themselves or to the purchasing units to carry out the evaluation. The method of evaluation can be characterized as very traditional. One of the most often used methods is controlling budget reports. Frequent meetings between the administration and the service institution are also a common way of evaluating the contract.

The data available can tell only a little about how the evaluations and contracts are used. The contracts (and the results of the evaluations) are primarily used to adjust the economic conditions for the contract, to adjust the political objectives, and as a tool for dialogue between the political level and the service institutions. Again, very few local governments use the evaluation results to benchmark.

DISCUSSION AND CONCLUSION

Performance contracting inside Danish local governments has caught on as a governance tool. Large municipalities use it more often than small municipalities; but based on the tremendous increase in the use of internal contracting over the past couple of years, it is likely to spread to all types of local governments. The use of internal contracting is apparently not related to municipalities led by liberal/conservative mayors or a function of prior use of reforms or management tools. This should also allow a more widespread use of internal contracting.

Purchase decisions and decisions to engage in contracting are primarily a matter for elite actors. Most employees are not included in the process. The use of internal contracting seems to be very pragmatic. Few municipalities use internal contracting across the board, and it is often implemented without reorganizing the administration in accordance with a provider-purchaser split model.

The question of whom to buy from is more restricted in the public sector, as many services are monopoly services. There is room for a light benchmarking also in the Danish case, but it is not used. Likewise, the use of internal markets is practically absent.

The question of what has been bought is handled by controlling performance measures and entering into a continuous dialogue with providers. Few local governments have established clear sanctions in case of contractual breach. The contractual governance model is thought of in input terms and governance terms, and less in control terms. If trouble or misbehavior should arise, dialogue will be the first tool to be used, not formal sanctions.

How can contractual governance function when there are few sanctions? One possible answer might be that contractual governance does not function. Governments are not getting a good deal on behalf of their citizens, because the provider organizations have incentives to cheat and not be detected. There will be a huge potential for rationalization if all tasks are examined closely. If sanctions are applied, there will be a boost in performance by public sector organizations. Another answer might be that contractual governance is thought of primarily as a governance model, not a control model. Danish local governments have been preoccupied with the potential for governance by input in contracts. The model is thought of not in control terms, but in governance terms. The way forward is to solve problems that may arise through dialogue. Dialogue is both a normative ideal and a guiding governance tool in the Danish public sector. If performance measures are not met, the purchaser will engage in a dialogue with the provider. If the provider thinks that resources could be used better another way, dialogue is the preferred mode of relating to the purchaser, not formal contractual negotiation.

This situation makes the Danish model of performance contracting potentially vulnerable. Yet reliance on soft contracting can also be an advantage in the long run, because contracting is institutionalized as a governance mechanism that provides a platform for dialogue between purchasers and internal providers. The existence of clear performance measures gives the dialogue a more secure platform. Contracting seems to be independent of the size or political affiliation of the local government, which enhances the prospects for contractual governance. Contractual governance seems to suit every type of local government, and more and more local governments are using it in Denmark. It seems to fit the administrative culture, and the absence of a traditional and formal contract culture can make way for a new and dialogue-based contract culture.

8

When Contractual Governance Fails

INTRODUCTION

Public-private partnerships (PPPs) have been hailed as the latest institutional form of cooperation between the public sector and the private sector (Savas 2000). PPPs can be defined as "cooperation of some durability between public and private actors in which they jointly develop products and services and share risks, costs and resources which are connected with these products or services" (Van Ham and Koppenjan 2001, 598). The institutional forms of PPPs vary from close contracting out cooperative efforts to infrastructure projects for building and operating new physical facilities such as schools, tunnels, bridges, or sports arenas. A PPP is still a "contested concept," with many different meanings attached to it (Linder 1999). PPPs are viewed by private companies as alternatives to "raw" contracting out (ISS 2002). Others view PPPs as financial arrangements whose utility for the public sector is difficult to see and which will exclude competition in the long run.

PPPs are only beginning to be used in public sectors around the globe. Most experience has been gathered in the U.K. (Institute of Public Policy Research 2000), the United States, and Australia, but other countries have followed suit (Osborne 2000). PPPs are mostly connected with experimental "front runner" or "best run" local governments that seek to explore new ways to deliver better public service to lower costs.

The local government of Farum in Denmark has been one of the world's most active local governments in experimenting with PPPs. In the early 1990s, Farum was among the candidates for the title of the "Best Run Local Government in the World" sponsored by the Bertelsmann Foundation in Germany. The winners were Phoenix, Arizona, and Christchurch, New Zealand. Since the 1980s, the charismatic mayor of Farum, Mr. Peter Brixtofte, has enjoyed an overall majority. Brixtofte has followed an active NPM/marketization strategy relying on contracting out and, later on, PPPs for delivery of public services. In 2000, Farum local government had contracted out its kindergartens and elder homes, made a sale-and-lease-back deal for its water supply and school buildings, and entered into BOOT (Build Own Operate Transfer, or Build Own Transfer) models for the construction of the sports arena, the Farum Arena, and the soccer stadium, Farum Park, as well as a nautical center called Farum Marina.

In early 2002, a major scandal erupted in Farum, with damaging consequences for the local government and its mayor. It was set off by newspaper revelations of excessive wine bills from restaurants, but soon grew much bigger. The "casualty list" from the scandal looks as follows: The mayor has been expelled from office. The local government is in effect administered economically by the Ministry of the Interior. Private companies paid money to the soccer club in exchange for securing contracts with the local government. Several investigations are going on, including a police investigation and a parliamentary commission. Farum has changed mayors three times since February 2002. The local government's finances are now in ruins, and local government taxes were raised by 3.2 percent in 2003. The former mayor faces criminal charges. The council will also face possible criminal charges because its members did not control the mayor's actions. The local chapter of the Liberal Party has been split into two separate chapters. The wider implications for local democracy in Denmark have yet to be considered.

The PPP deal is at the heart of the matter. It was the PPP deal for the construction of the soccer stadium and the sports arena, and the missing money from those deals, that triggered the development that led to the mayor's fall and the local government scandal. This chapter examines the following questions: Why did PPPs fail in Farum? What are the lessons from Farum for future PPP deals?

The main argument here is that a contractual governance perspective will help us to understand why the local government scandal took place. Managing a wide range of contracts is complicated. The mayor and the local council must know what they want to buy and whom to buy from, and be able to judge what they have bought. The structure of the contractual governance scheme in Farum was too complex for the mayor to oversee. Therefore, an important lesson to be learned from the Farum case is to make PPP deals more transparent and to involve the relevant stakeholders more. However, PPPs were a new arrangement, both politically and legally, for the central government to handle. Central government rules may not be adequate for new experimenting local governments like Farum. There is also an important lesson here to be learned for central government, which is to be better prepared and to prepare the legislation for innovative local governments. When the central government did act, it acted more or less in panic and simply stopped the PPP deals overnight.

THE RISKS AND PROMISES OF PUBLIC-PRIVATE PARTNERSHIPS

The term *PPP* can be defined in broad terms or in narrower terms. In broad terms, it simply means any form of cooperation between organizations in the public sector and the private sector, usually meaning "cooperative ventures between the state and private business" (Linder, 1999, 35). Contracting out can be viewed as a form of PPP from this perspective (Savas 2000). A narrower conception will look at PPPs as distinct from contracting out. Contracting out means a principal-agent relationship between public purchasers and private providers. The relationship is characterized by mistrust, as principals and agents both seem to maximize their utility. Contracts are usually for shorter periods, of a maximum of five years. PPP means cooperation based on trust, where the parties to the contract are on equal terms. Contract periods are long-term, sometimes up to 30 or more years. PPPs have the following elements: a businesslike relationship, common decision-making procedures, risk sharing, and long-term contractual relations. A PPP can be defined as "cooperation of some durability between public and private actors in which they jointly develop products and services and share risks, costs and resources which are connected with these products or services" (Van Ham and Koppenjan 2001, 598). PPPs focus on the cooperation of entities: "The hallmark of partnerships is cooperation, not competition; the disciplining mechanism is not customer exit or thin profit margins, but a joint venture that spreads financial risk between private and private sectors" (Linder 1999, 35).

The institutional form of a PPP varies. It can be a formal joint-venture company, an agreement to cooperate, or simply a new organization in which both public and private parties participate. Some include cooperation between public organizations and voluntary organizations as distinct forms of partnerships (Salamon 1995). Savas (2000) lists a number of possible types of PPPs, including infrastructure projects like BOOT, BOT, BOO, and other models. These highly complex models rest on extensive risk sharing between the parties in the partnership.

Central to the definition and understanding of PPPs is risk sharing. The parties to the contract are interested in gain sharing (Domberger 1998), and they cannot specify all future requirements in a contract. The partnership contract is therefore a relational contract in Williamson's (1996) sense of the term. Some points must be left open to future negotiation as new contingencies arise. Public organizations must confront a number of risks when they enter a PPP: substantive risks, financial risks, risks of private discontinuity, democratic risks, and political risks (Van Ham and Koppenjan 2001, 599–602). Public organizations must beware that private parties do not transfer their own financial risks to the public sector. Another risk for the public organization is not being able to understand the complex financial deals that private parties present to the public sector. Likewise, private parties run risks, especially by entering into a contract with a politically led organization, which may have new leadership by the next local council election.

If there are risks, why consider entering into a PPP? PPPs hold certain promises for local governments. The first promise is that a PPP will limit the local government's financial situation, either by injecting cash into the local government's finances or by providing capital that can be used to build or construct new physical facilities for the use of the local government's citizens. The second promise is that public services can be delivered more effectively and at a lower price. This is of course a highly debatable point. Third, PPPs promise that innovation of public service delivery will take place. Access to the expertise of the private sector will be provided through the use of PPPs. For the private parties, the attraction lies in gaining new markets and getting new investment opportunities (Van Ham and Koppenjan 2001, 597). Risk management is a central part of any PPP arrangement, and the partners to the contract must recognize the risks involved, try to reduce them, and allocate the risks to the parties most prepared to take them on (Van Ham and Koppenjan 2001, 601).

PPPs as infrastructure projects have been criticized from several perspectives. First, is the meaning of local government to "manage risk"? Too much entrepreneurship in government may not suit the democratic and legal foundation upon which the public sector is founded (Terry 1998). Traditionally, public bureaucracy has been risk-averse almost by definition. Equality before the law, fair treatment for all, and legally based decision making have been hallmarks of what has been called "the traditional model of public administration" (Hughes 1998). The point is that local governments should avoid risk-related projects and stick to traditional and competent administration. Risk taking is for private sector companies and not local governments. Second, the democratic accountability of PPPs is not sufficiently worked out yet. "The deal" in PPP arrangements is not easily made transparent (Hodge 2002). How can a mayor and a local council entering into a 20- or 30-year contract be held accountable? What the mayor does is to constrain future mayors and local council members in their decision-making capabilities. Third, the financial and juridical elements are complex and require insight from a legal perspective or a financial analysis perspective. Should the future of local government finances be taken out of traditional economists' hands and be given to contract lawyers and financial investment experts?

PUBLIC-PRIVATE PARTNERSHIPS IN FARUM AND THE SCANDAL IN 2002

PPPs in Farum

Use of PPPs in the broad sense of the term has been a key strategy for Farum local government since the early 1990s. Contracting out has been used extensively. Farum contracted out its kindergartens and elder homes to the Danish international company ISS. In the late 1990s, Farum local government was the first local government in Denmark to contract out administrative work at the city hall to a private company (one of the big five auditing companies). In one of the several books the mayor has written (Brixtofte 2000), the policy of contracting out and PPPs was hailed as revolutionary in a Danish public service context.

PPPs in the narrow sense of infrastructure projects and deals have been used since the mid-1990s in Farum. Sale-and-lease-back was a preferred policy instrument. The local government sold its water company, wastewater facilities, schools, and swimming pools and leased them back. In 2000 the Ministry of the Interior put a stop to the sale-and-lease-back arrangements.

The mayor pushed forward three big construction projects in the late 1990s: a 3,500 capacity indoor sports arena (Farum Arena), a state-of-the-art soccer stadium (Farum Park), and a nautical marina (Farum Marina). The financing of the projects came from private financial sources. The main financial institution was the FIH Institute, which financed all three major infrastructure projects. The deal was that Farum would obtain loans; FIH would build, own, and operate the facilities and turn the facilities over to the Farum local government after 20 years. The great discussion among politicians, administrators, and citizens has been about what financial risks are involved in the deal. Opinions were divided into two camps: Farum local government executives (foremost the mayor, who was enthusiastic about the idea and who had the support of his majority party) and the political opposition in Farum plus skeptical citizens' groups. Business magazines also have been skeptical and have examined the foundations of the deal and found them fragile at best. In a now-famous passage, an editorial in *Børsens Nyhedsmagasin* accused the mayor of gambling in the casino with taxpayers' money (an accusation that was dismissed by the mayor and his adviser at the time).

The Development of the Farum Scandal

On February 6, 2002, the daily tabloid newspaper *BT* carried a headline story on its front page announcing that mayor Peter Brixtofte of Farum had been picking up huge restaurant bills for red wine, at over 8,000 DKK a bottle. One bill alone listed "red wine" for 64,000 DKK for the mayor and four of his friends for one evening. Numerous newspaper stories of the Farum experiment had run in newspapers before that, but no other story had produced "hard evidence." *BT* had hard evidence in the form of the restaurant bills and witness statements from former employees of the restaurant. Among politicians and journalists, the drinking habits of Peter Brixtofte had been widely known, but few had acted upon the knowledge, for example, by publicly telling Brixtofte to quit drinking. At first, therefore, it seemed like "a good news story," but nothing more. In the following weeks, the scandal grew at a rapid pace. Further investigations showed that the local government had paid excessive bills that were actually connected to the soccer club, of which the mayor was also chairman and shareholder. A civil servant in Farum then disclosed—moved by the opportunity to tell other mismanagement stories—that he had been forced to withhold a payment for a building site in Farum, which triggered a bonus check for 325,000 DKK to a close friend of the mayor. According to the civil servant, the mayor had made a clear decision and ordered the civil servant to withhold the payment so a check would be issued.

Around the same time, the Complaints Council for Contracting Out announced that the tender process in which FIH had won the right to finance the infrastructure projects of the soccer stadium and the sports arena had not followed EU rules on tender and contracting out. Farum had claimed it was not the owner of the facilities because FIH had taken them over in the PPP deal. FIH as the owner was not obliged to follow the EU tender rules. But the Complaints Council for Contracting Out ruled that Farum was, in effect, still the owner (because FIH was not allowed to make alterations to the facilities without the consent of Farum local government). A relatively huge sum of money had to be deposited. Farum local government was not allowed to use the money in its daily running of the local government. Technically speaking, this was not a "sale-and-lease-back" arrangement, although it has been called that in the media and by the Complaints Council for Contracting Out. Instead, the construction of Farum Arena and parts of Farum Park was another type of PPP— the "build-own-operate-transfer (BOOT)" model. Farum had sold the ground where Farum Arena was to stand. FIH built the sports arena, owns it, and is to operate it until—in 20 years' time—it will be transferred to

Farum local government. FIH finances the deal through a 20-year loan, but Farum local government has to fund it through its lease of the facilities. Because the Complaints Council ruled that it was not legal according to EU tender rules, the claim from the citizen who made the case is that 20 percent could have been saved (the rule of thumb for contracting out savings). That is disputed by Hodge (2000), whose analysis shows that savings are not that high. The loan could have been 20 percent cheaper if the claim is true.

This piece of news came at a particularly bad time for Farum, as the mayor had recently bought a discontinued army base with the intention of turning it into profitable new housing estates. The mayor needed the money from the PPP deal with the private financial company because it would take some time to construct and sell the housing estates.

When all this took place, the mayor was in the Canary Islands in Spain, where he was taking a holiday. On February 7, 2002, the day after the "red wine story," the mayor took sick leave, and on February 8, he flew to the Canary Islands. On the Canary Island of Lanzarote, friends surrounded him, as senior citizens in Farum had been given a free trip to the Canary Islands. In the newspaper, *BT*, it was revealed how the senior citizens' trips became "money machines" for the local government, because the travel company paid for sponsorships to the soccer club, where the mayor was chairman. The press soon flew out, and for a week, Brixtofte conducted interviews and commented on the situation back in Farum from the poolside of his hotel in the Canary Islands (until his attorney advised him to come home and face the allegations and his critics).

The scandal evolved in a number of surprising ways. The papers of the civil servant who had complained about the mayor were removed when the head of the mayor's secretariat, Steen Gennsmann, on February 10, broke into the office of the civil servant in the middle of the night, in true Watergate style, and removed a number of papers and filing reports that were the proof material. On the evening of February 11, the police began an action in which the town hall was ransacked and more than 50 removal boxes full of paper were taken away, as well as several computers. On February 14, it was revealed how the Farum local government charged too high prices from companies involved in the infrastructure projects, only to transfer the money to the local soccer club.

On February 18, it was revealed that the mayor had secured a bank loan of 250 million DKK without consulting the local council. Allegedly, the local government's debt had grown so much that the payment of salaries to the employees in Farum local government had been at stake. At first, the mayor denied that he had secured the loan, but later on, the fact was confirmed. Later in February, it was disclosed that the mayor and his chief administrative officer had paid up to 9 million DKK to a close friend of the mayor in the building industry.

The Ministry of Interior took no action in the first days of the scandal. But on February 20, the minister announced that he would put the Farum local government "under administration" because of the disastrous economic situation. The decision was verified in the spring. A twist to the minister's ruling is that the minister is a former ally of the mayor. They belong to the same party, and they both encouraged market solutions for the public sector. The minister was previously vice-mayor in a local government in the same region in Denmark as Farum. Prior to becoming minister, he was mayor of the regional government of Frederiksborg (where Farum local government is situated).

On March 21, the mayor was finally suspended from office, after lengthy negotiations on how to construct a suspension and who would replace him. The cause cited was the bank loan of 250 million DKK, which the mayor had not told the local council about. A new mayor, Paul Watchell, from a Citizens' List, replaced Brixtofte as mayor, but only for a short while. In his absence, Henrik Jerner, a liberal party member, was stand-in mayor in February for a short period. The Minister of the Interior confirmed the suspension of Mr. Brixtofte as mayor on May 6, 2002.

As a result of the economic transactions and the disastrous economic situation, the minister also confirmed Farum's local council's decision to raise personal income tax by 3.2 percent for 2003. Farum local government had gone from being one of the cheapest local governments to live under to being one of the most expensive in Denmark.

Various investigations have been launched into the Farum scandal:

1. The police are investigating the mayor's actions. Charges have been brought against the mayor for unlawfully obtaining a bank loan without the knowledge or the consent of the local council.
2. An attorney investigation is examining whether anything illegal has been happening in the transactions of the local government in Farum.
3. The opposition parties in the Danish Parliament pushed for a parliamentary "investigating commission," which was to begin its work in 2003. The purpose of the commission is to make sure that no stone is left unturned in the investigation of what happened in Farum, with the explicit aim of preventing similar scandals in the future (Forslag til Folketingsbeslutning om Undersøgelseskommission om Farum, 1. Behandling 20. November 2002 i Folketinget).
4. A special committee appointed by the Minister of the Interior and chaired by a university professor, Mr. Jens Peter Christensen, has examined the role of the local council and the regulatory mechanisms for local governments in the wake of the Farum scandal. The committee came up with 17 proposals, which were to be translated into Danish law during 2003.

As of July 2003, Mr. Brixtofte was facing the following charges: (1) a charge for violating § 55 of the Danish Law on Punishment for having agreed to a loan for the local government without consulting the local council, (2) charges for swindling with mandates (including securing money for business partners), and (3) misuse of authority as mayor (including not monitoring the development of excessive costs to the local government). If convicted, the mayor could face prison. In addition, the members of the local council may face penalties for not having secured control of the economic situation. Brixtofte's former chief administrative officer is also facing charges (*Politiken*, May 16, 2003: 23 på anklagebænken).

WHEN PUBLIC-PRIVATE PARTNERSHIPS FAIL: LESSONS FROM FARUM

PPPs in Farum have failed in the sense that because one arrangement was found in violation of EU regulations for tender and contracting out, the government (the Ministry of the Interior) effectively banned the sale-and-lease-back arrangements in Farum's version. Neither type of PPP arrangement is working as first intended by the local government. In contracting out, private sector providers paid for sponsorships for the soccer team in exchange for contracts for public service delivery. When ISS declined to pay for sponsorships for the soccer club, the mayor stopped cooperating with ISS as a contractor for the local government's kindergartens. In a wider perspective, PPPs have contributed to a low morale in the local government.

Referring to points introduced in the theory section, the next section looks at risk taking and regulation (risk taking without constraints or risk taking in a regulated environment?), the nature of the PPP deals (simple or complex?), and democratic accountability (clear accountability structure or insufficient accountability structure?).

Clashes between Central Rules and Local Innovation

When Farum began sale-and-lease-back arrangements, the concept was very unfamiliar in the Ministry of the Interior and in the State Regulation Council that regulates local government affairs. Suddenly, Farum had all this money in its hands, which it could use to purchase new public services. The Ministry looked upon the activities with some bewilderment. Gradually, the thought dawned on the Ministry that sale-and-lease-back arrangements could be a potential danger to national economic policy if local governments were allowed to sell and then lease back their physical assets. Too many local governments in too much debt could destabilize the economy. More and more local governments were beginning to follow Farum's model in the 1990s. The daily newspaper *Politiken* counted 13 local governments that had experimented with PPPs. The Ministry of the Interior decided in the end that it would not allow sale-and-lease-back arrangements as Farum had introduced them. Instead, local governments had to place the money from sale-and-lease-back arrangements effectively in escrow, making it indifferent to the local government whether or not to pursue sale-and-lease-back arrangements. This is a case where central rules were not up to date or geared for an innovative practice in local governments. Instead of designing new rules to meet the challenge of PPP arrangements, the central government responded with a preemptive strike, essentially to forbid the kind of arrangements that Farum was promoting.

In the case of the BOOT model for constructing the new indoor sports arena and the soccer stadium, central rules again collided with new local government practice. Farum local government had signed a contract with a financial institution (called FIH) that gave FIH the right to a green field site in the city of Farum, with a clause saying that FIH should construct a new indoor stadium. In another contract, the construction of the new part of the soccer stadium was also handed over to FIH. The controversial issue in this case was whether Farum local government had thereby violated the EU tender and contracting out rules because the contract was not put out to tender. In Farum's argument, the local government was not responsible for constructing the sports arena or the stadium, but had left it to FIH to do the work. The missing part is the bidding process. We cannot know if Farum could have got the sports arena and soccer stadium for a cheaper price, because the contract was not put out to tender. Again we see a clash between centrally laid-out rules and new local government practice. In this case, the rules for EU tender are reasonably clear, and it could be argued (as the Complaints Council did in its ruling) that Farum was, in effect, the owner of the sports arena and soccer stadium and that therefore this bending of the rules was not acceptable.

The two cases raise broader questions of the central government rules and the new local government practices with PPPs. It shows that the rules are not designed for PPP arrangements. PPP arrangements either have to be fitted into the traditional set of rules (in the case of EU tender rules) or have to be evaluated in no particular context when central government has no previous position or ruling to rely on (in the case of the sale-and-lease-back arrangement).

The former mayor of Farum has made the argument several times that the regulatory system is not sufficiently prepared to deal with local governments that introduce new practices in public service delivery. The mayor is right in saying that adequate regulation is missing. However, this is no excuse for violating existing rules.

"Closed deals" and Missing Transparency in Local Government

The second point relates to the nature of the contract that Farum local government entered into with the financial institution FIH and other contractors. Farum did not follow an open-door policy. Access to relevant documents was hard to get for the opposition in the local councils, for citizens' groups, and for journalists. The mayor was not forthcoming in revealing the details and conditions of the contracts that he as mayor signed on behalf of the local councils. The financial and juridical implications of the deals were not clear.

In 1999, the newsmagazine *Børsens Nyhedsmagasin* tried to assess the risk Farum was taking with the new PPP arrangements. The mayor and his economic adviser defended their contractual construction vigorously. The newsmagazine, in an article as well as in an editorial, claimed that the calculations and the financial forecasts were not safe and that the mayor was, in effect, gambling with (future) taxpayers' money. For nonfinancial experts, the argument was hard to follow, as it mainly concerned the judgment of future rent developments. These are highly detailed and complex financial arguments, and only a handful of financial experts would be able to penetrate the logic and the construction of the financial PPP arrangements.

Lack of Attention to Democratic Accountability

The third point is that democratic accountability was not considered properly in the Farum case. The mayor had in the past been formally accountable to the local council. In local governments, the prospect of being ousted from office by the voters on Election Day has been the primary mechanism of effective democratic control. But since the mayor enjoyed an overall majority in several periods in office and had many loyal followers and admirers, the party's councilors did not question the thinking behind the PPP deals. Formal democratic accountability within the local council was not effective in regulating the behavior of the mayor and holding him to account for his actions in the Farum case.

Other institutions of democratic control through auditing, ombudsman control, and regulation of local government activities were neglected in Farum to a certain extent. The bodies the mayor had to account to have not lived up to their responsibilities. The auditor who audited the finances of local governments did not detect any wrongdoing or mismanagement in its accountancy reports. The other regulatory body is the State Regulatory Council, a central government institution that regionally has a duty to oversee matters and regulate at the local government level. Despite many expressions of concern from citizens and citizens' groups, the State

Regulatory Council was not able to correct the mismanagement and wrong-doing in Farum. Only recently has the Ombudsman, the nation's watchman for public affairs, been allowed to handle local government issues.

The auditing institutions at the local level and the regulatory system were undergoing change or preparing for change while Farum local government experimented with PPPs. Administrative audit ("forvaltningsrevision") only recently has been made compulsory for local governments (it has been a feature in the audit of central government for years). Administrative audit at that time had not found a position in local government. However, the financial audit should have detected some of the problems (including unlawfully obtaining bank loans). In the case of the State Regulatory Council, a government white paper has critiqued the regulation of local governments, and the government has for some time advocated an overhaul of the regulatory structure. In effect, various ministers who made it clear they wanted a new regulatory structure have undermined the work of the State Regulatory Council, which has not enjoyed sufficient legitimacy for several years. This situation made it easier for the mayor to dismiss the rulings and judgments of the State Regulatory Council (why take its rulings seriously if it is going to be abolished anyway?). Farum local government exploited the gap in the regulatory system by pushing forward with reforms that no institution was able to evaluate properly because of insufficient expert knowledge and no standing.

Low Ethics in the Conduct of Public Service

There is a wider issue that goes beyond the breaking or bending of existing rules. Did partnerships and contracting that implied detailed negotiations with private sector companies lead to low ethical standards and consequently to unacceptable and unethical behavior on the part of the mayor and his close advisers? There is an argument to be made that extensive use of PPPs will lead to overly close connections between local governments and private providers.

In the case of Farum, the mayor built up close relationships with private providers of public services in the areas of kindergartens and elder homes. Negotiations with private providers meant many meetings and close dealings. To secure a contract, company executives might be willing to engage in new relationships. In the Farum case, private providers agreed to pay sponsor fees to the soccer club in exchange for contracts with the local government.

With the infrastructure PPP arrangements, Farum built a close relationship with the financial institution FIH, which provided the financing for Farum's big projects, the sports arena and the soccer stadium. The Complaints Council's decision showed that the relationship was too close for comfort and that Farum should have put the tender out to the open market.

The implication of the argument is that close negotiations for public service delivery for longer periods of time can make the relationship between public sector organizations and private sector organizations too close, risking abuse toward citizens and taxpayers. As Adam Smith once noted, if you put too many people of one profession together in a room, it will not be long before they put their own interests before that of the general public.

Against this argument is the fact that the mayor had been in office since the 1980s and had enjoyed an overall majority. "Power corrupts," and the mayor had simply been too long in office. The Farum scandal had more to do with traditional power politics than with PPPs and contracting. The mayor would have shown similar behavior even if Farum had not collaborated with the financial institution to construct the new stadium.

CONCLUSION

This chapter considers the spectacular scandal in the Danish local government of Farum in Denmark, which evolved during 2002 and continues to amaze the public, public administrators, and politicians. The scandal is also an embarrassment to the national government, which is promoting marketization and partnerships with the private sector as a key part of its policy program (Regeringen 2002). First, the Farum case has shown that infrastructure PPPs lead to a potential clash between local government ambitions and central government rules. Before adequate legislation is in place, PPPs are likely to lead to failure in the sense that they cannot be carried out as planned by local governments. Second, the Farum case shows that the financial deals behind infrastructure PPPs are complex and require financial expertise to judge whether the deals are healthy for the local government economy. PPPs involve risks and need a risk management effort. In the long run, it is debatable if the fate of local government economy should be left to financial analysts instead of political judgment. Third, the Farum case shows that democratic accountability is fragile in PPPs. Democratic accountability cannot rely solely on election days, but must be supplemented by renewed democratic institutions of control such as auditing, the ombudsman, and the regulatory council. All these institutions must be prepared for local governments that are not only traditional administrative units, but also risk-taking, innovative, managerial-minded local governments. The control side has to be as dynamic as the innovative side of local government activity. The policy implication is that PPPs must be treated with care.

What does the future hold for PPPs? Several authors have noted how a lack of competition is unhealthy for public-private cooperation. Van Ham and Koppenjan (2001, 606) ask "how to retain competition in partnership without lapsing into contracting out." One strategy could be to try "serial organizational monogamy" (Greve and Ejersbo 2002). Serial organizational monogamy describes a relationship between public and private organizations that is built on trust, but for only a limited period of time. The main challenge of PPPs in their current form is that they are set to last too many years (20 to 50 years), which is difficult to work with for public managers and politicians who usually have much shorter time spans on their mind. Serial organizational monogamy means that public sector organizations and private sector organizations can cooperate—and even enter into institutional forms of partnerships—but not necessarily until "death do them part"—or, rather, till the contract expires. The contract horizon must be much more focused for public managers and politicians to work with it. As companies start to refer to "raw contracting out" (as is the case with Danish-based ISS) when they want to engage in long-term partnerships with local governments, the local governments must be aware of the danger of tying oneself to one professional partner for too long a time, which will squeeze out competition. For a market to work, there must be some sort of competition, or at least the prospect of competition. The right way for local governments is to acknowledge that a partnership can take place, but also to make it clear that competitors are waiting in the wings if the partnership does not turn out as planned. Serial organizational monogamy can be a viable alternative to both traditional contracting out and new arrangements with partnerships.

9

Conclusion: Contractual Governance in a Cross-Cultural Perspective

INTRODUCTION

Contracting has come a long way since the early 1970s and is now an established feature of most national and local governments. Contracting is considered a tool among other tools. Contracting fits into the New Public Management reforms that have swept the world's governments (Fortin and van Hassel 2000). What contracting is not is a tool to cure all malfunctions in government. Observers and scholars frequently stress that contracting must not be seen as tool that all reform types can revolve around (Domberger 1998; Hodge 2000). Contracting has become another well-established and respected tool among all the tools that governments can use to make their services work better and cost less.

CONTRACTING AS REINVENTED INSTITUTIONS

The book uses Kettl's model of the contracting process as a point of departure. Kettl (1993) posed three questions that a contracting organization must face. What to buy? Whom to buy from? What has been bought? We added a fourth question that precedes the three other questions (Why buy?). From Kettl's work, we outlined a model that follows the phases and added the different contracting forms: internal performance-based contracting, contracting out, and public-private partnerships. The under-lying governance structure of each model is hierarchy, market, and net-work governance. The nature of the contract itself has also been examined. There are two dimensions to every contract: a soft dimension and a hard dimension. Most contracts are built around a "hard" base and topped up with a "soft" dimension. The conceptualization of the nature of man can also differ. Using March and Olsen's concepts, we have talked about a logic of consequentiality (utility-maximizing individuals) and a logic of appropriateness (norm-following individuals). Knowing from what dimension of contracting and what model of human nature an organiza-tion is working is important to understand how contracting works.

The first finding is that contracting out continues to be on the policy agenda. Contracting out is a subject that refuses to go away. There will always be a new case that is judged either as successful or as a failure. There will always be politicians who are willing to step forward and sug-gest new contracting out initiatives. There will always be worker unions that will seek to protect their members' working conditions and relate to contracting out from that perspective. And there will always be public managers struggling to make all the various objectives transform into a coherent policy that will be possible to manage.

Different advocacy coalitions propose or oppose contracting out. In chapter 4, the analytical tools of the Advocacy Coalition Framework (ACF) were used to examine contracting out policy in Denmark in the period 1995–2000. In our analysis, we assumed that there were two coali-tions, a "pro-coalition" and an "anti-coalition." The analysis showed that there is a need for a more sophisticated picture. At least four different coalitions were identified. The most radical coalitions on both sides are hard to get to the negotiation table. The radical coalitions will keep on agi-tating from their various perspectives. In the ACF, the coalitions are assumed to have "deep core beliefs" that cannot be transformed unless under extreme circumstances. It seems fair to say that some of the coali-tions hold deep core beliefs about the advantage of either the private sec-tor or the public sector in public service delivery. Their attitudes toward contracting out are not likely to change. What is argued in the ACF is that technical information can play a role in changing the attitudes of the other coalitions' beliefs. Secondary beliefs can be changed if the technical infor-mation is persuasive enough. Debating technical information takes place in professional forums and through policy reports on contracting out that tackle technical issues head on. A technical issue may be how to write a contract to specify all the desired objectives correctly. If a local govern-ment has not written a contract for human services before, the local gov-ernment needs technical information on how to set performance targets and how to write them into the contract. The problem can be addressed in reports, by consultants, and through the exchange of information with other local governments that have previous experience in contracting. The theory then assumes that the local government can learn how to write the contract and thereby be better at doing contracting out in the future. The condition for learning is that professional forums exist and that reports are written that are easily accessible. A wide range of problems or challenges connected to contracting out might be confronted through a learning process, the ACF assumes.

The analysis showed that although many cases have been debated and many reports have been issued, the advocacy coalitions for and against contracting out have not revised their perspectives on contracting out dramatically. The anti-coalition has become more positive toward contracting out during the five-year period examined. But the pro-coalition has not waived its perspectives and is still advocating contracting out. It could be concluded that contracting out is about persuading or changing the attitudes of the anti-coalition so that they become more favorable to contracting out. Contracting out policy is perhaps more subtle than that. The problems change all the time. Another interpretation of the development could be that contracting out will continue to be controversial for some time. There are no "quick fixes" or heaps of technical information waiting to be spread, digested, and implemented. It can be difficult to find out what kind of information is "technical" and what kind of information is political. The type of cases that get propelled into the public debate is hard to predict or to control.

The second finding concerns the contracting process. The analysis of the literature on contracting in the United States and Scandinavia, the case studies on local government contracting in Odense and Dane County, and the survey on performance-based contracting in Denmark point to a reformulation of the elements in the Kettl model.

There is a need to rethink the purchaser function (the "what to buy" question). In the Kettl model, the purchaser function is important because governments must learn how to be smart buyers. In our analysis we found that local governments in the United States have become smart buyers to a certain extent. Managers are trained to become contract managers. There is an elaborate performance target–setting culture that allows governments to specify what they want to buy. But purchasing is also a function that depends on advice, negotiations, and discussions with other organizations. In the Dane County case, the local government consults with the provider organizations (purchase of service agencies) on what to buy. Knowledge about what to buy comes from the provider organizations. In Scandinavia, organizations enlist consultants to help with formulating contracts. Formally, the decision to contract out remains with the chief administrative officer or the local government council, but the decision is a result of many organizations' inputs. We should therefore amend the purchasing role and suggest a new formulation: What to buy is a process shared by a number of actors, including to some extent provider organizations because they know about the details of the service.

There is a need to rethink the provider function (the "whom to buy from" question). In contracting out theory, it is assumed that governments have specified what they want to buy and then look for some providers that will adhere to the demands of the purchaser. The analysis has confirmed a picture already widespread, that providers come in many shapes and forms.

The first division is between for-profit providers (private companies) and nonprofit providers (usually charities or voluntary organizations). In the United States, there is a much greater variety of providers to choose from. In the United States, nonprofit organizations are very prolific compared to the Scandinavian experience. Nonprofit organizations have a long history of providing public service. What is more striking is that nonprofit organizations are still developing themselves and finding new ways of making alliances. Nonprofit organizations frequently enter into partnerships or consortiums that can become innovative service providers. This has been seen in Wisconsin, but also in other parts of the country, for example, in New York City. The Scandinavian countries still rely to a great extent on private for-profit companies when the local governments contract out. This picture may change in the future, but it is a fact now that nonprofit organizations do not have the same experience in providing public services through contracting arrangements.

The second division is between the territories of the providers. Some providers may act locally and are based locally. In Dane County, Wisconsin, there are a lot of small, local providers of human services. Some providers, however, operate nationally. This goes for Maximus Inc., which operates in a number of states in the United States. Maximus is a nonprofit organization that has contracts for services in many states. In Denmark, the company Falck is providing ambulance services to many Danish local governments. Finally, some companies operate internationally or globally. Falck, for example, is a part of the global firm Group 4 Falck, which operates in the United States, Scandinavia, Australia, and many other places. Some providers are dependent on local governments. In Dane County, many of the small, local nonprofits are totally dependent on the Department of Human Services for their existence. What is happening with providers recently is that local or central governments may become dependent on providers as well. The providers that operate services may be crucial to the local or national community; if they were to withdraw from the market, it would be a difficult situation for the local government.

The North American scholar Alasdair Roberts (2002) talks about "a subscriber state." In this vision, governments around the world will increasingly subscribe to standardized services provided by service providers operating nationally or globally. These service providers are so huge and have such dominant market positions that governments often will have little choice but to subscribe to the available services. While the vision is probably far from being a reality yet, the concept of the subscriber state may point to situations where governments will at least be as dependent on the providers as the providers are on the governments. The concept of the subscriber state indicates that governments will not always be able to be "smart buyers" if the providers are even smarter! For many local governments, it will be a problem if they cannot specify the services they want. Politically, that can disappoint the voters. Politicians often advocate contracting out on the basis that governments are able to specify exactly what kind of service they want delivered from the private sector. Small local governments may not be in a position to put demands forward in "the subscriber state." Local governments will then have to join forces to match the market power of the bigger providers. In Denmark, the current effort to reform the local governments to make them into bigger units can be seen in this perspective: Bigger local governments may have more bargaining power and expertise against increasingly competent providers that operate nationally and globally, not just locally. In the Kettl model, there is a need to reformulate the provider position so that providers can have both national and global aspirations that must be taken into consideration by the local governments.

There is a need to rethink the accountability issue (the "what has been bought" question). Generally, our analysis has shown that governments are becoming better and more sophisticated in measuring service provider performance. In Dane County, Wisconsin, an elaborate and detailed monitoring and control system is institutionalized. There is a system for performance measurement and a separate system for dealing with complaints and grievances. There is also a system for dealing with breaks in contractual obligations. Everything is taken care of and specified in the contract. The difficult part in the Wisconsin case is to terminate contracts because cooperation between purchasers and providers is institutionalized and because most of the providers have friends in high political places they can mobilize if necessary. The accountability system involves hierarchical, legal, professional, and political accountability (Romzek 1998).

The accountability system has become more and more sophisticated. Often it will start from a performance measurement system. It will also include juridical accountability if matters cannot be settled. In addition to the more formalized systems, local governments are building continuing relationships with providers. In Dane County, the Department of Human Services is in close contact with all providers and meets with a group of the bigger providers on a regular basis. These meetings are designed to deal with problems that may occur and to discuss future challenges and new solutions. In Scandinavia, local governments and companies alike are eager to build dialogue mechanisms into the contractual relationships. Although many Scandinavian local governments that contract out still look at performance indicators, some local governments, such as Grested-Gilleleje, have built dialogue meetings into their relationships with the providers. For Kettl's model, there is a need to recognize that in some local governments, evaluation, control, and accountability appear to have reached a mature level at the present time (Table 9.1).

The third finding relates to the composition of the contract itself. We have distinguished between a hard dimension and a soft dimension of a contract. We have also made a distinction between a utility-maximizing

TABLE 9.1
The Contractual Governance Model Revisited

	Kettl model	Redefined model
Why buy?	Not considered specifically	Many arguments put forward; still an emphasis on ideology and saving costs despite claim for pragmatism
What to buy?	Governments learn how to be smart buyers	Purchasing a function of input from a number of actors, including consultants and providers
Whom to buy from?	Variety of providers both profit and nonprofit	Variety of providers both profit and nonprofit. Providers also vary according to the market aspirations; local, national, or global. Increasing trend of international or global-oriented providers, which can be difficult to match for local governments.
What has been bought?	Governments need to have accountability system in place	Elaborate and sophisticated accountability mechanisms have become institutionalized, especially in U.S. local governments. Include performance measurements, and redress possibilities, but also dialogue and informal relationships of shared forums between purchasers and providers.

actor (logic of consequentiality) and a norm-following actor (logic of appropriateness). The analysis shows that both dimensions of contracts are used in local governments, and both types of actor models are followed in local governments. The hard dimension of a contract can be seen as a sort of base contract. The softer dimension is then built on top of that base. Most local governments will have what we define as a hard contract. In the Dane County case, there is clearly a hard type of contract. But the contract depends on the softer dimension of the contract: The actors need to know about each others' motives and policies. How the actors are conceived of is another question. Here, there does not seem to be a uniform picture. Actors follow incentives, which points to the logic of consequentiality. But actors also conform to the norms that surround the contracting process, which points to the logic of appropriateness.

Contracts have a hard dimension and a soft dimension. Contracts are built on legal basis, but need the informal institutional arrangements as well to work properly. As Durkheim said, not everything in a contract can be contractualized. Contracts operate with an incentive-based notion of actors and a norm-based notion of actors. Hard-based incentives are backed up by norm-following incentives. In individual contracts and individual contractual relationships, the point is to find the mix between hard and soft contracts and hard and soft incentives.

In local governments in the United States, the mix points toward more hard contracts coupled with soft contracts and a preference for hard-based incentives backed up with negotiated agreements that prescribe norms that actors are bound to follow if the contractual relationship is to run smoothly. In local governments in Scandinavia, the mix points to softer contracts that are nevertheless still based on hard contracts. A lot of new contracts will try to simulate the harder type of contract to make themselves look like market arrangements. The incentives are also a mix of negotiated, norm-following incentives increasingly being backed by more hard-based incentives wired into the contracts. The United States and Scandinavia do not seem to be that far apart in contractual conceptualization.

When contracts fail, it might be that the type of contract does not fit with the existing, or presumed, model of individual action behavior. A hard-based contract will have a difficult implementation stage if actors are following other norms and do not respond to the incentives set up in the contract. Likewise, a softer, looser contract may not be a success if the actors it is supposed to govern are behaving in a utility-maximizing manner, thereby undermining the foundations of the contract. In Denmark, performance-based contracts presuppose that actors will concur with the prevailing norms in the public sector. If actors become hard-edged utility maximization agents, the model is likely to break down because, for an example, no specific sanctions are tied to the contract. In the United States, if a local government only set up a loose contractual framework, more

TABLE 9.2
Contractual Governance in a Cross-Cultural Perspective

	Hard	*Soft*
Logic of consequentiality	U.S. local governments outset position. Scandinavian extended position.	Scandinavian extended position.
Logic of appropriateness	U.S. local government extended position.	U.S. local government extended position. Scandinavian outset position. Scandinavian performance-based contracting.

hard-based utility maximizing providers would see their way to get better deals for themselves and thereby might neglect their primary customers. Matching contracts and assumed behavior of agents is one of the key challenges for designers of contractual institutional arrangements (Table 9.2).

The fourth finding concerns the contract culture. Evidently, the contract culture is an important factor in the analysis, but how important it is is very difficult to estimate. We have tried to assess the role of the contract culture (Table 9.3). It seems clear that some local governments in the United States have a much longer history of contracting than some of the local governments in Scandinavia. Contracting is wired into the relationships between purchasers and providers in the United States. The regulatory aspects are confirmed and institutionalized in contractual documents. In Dane County, and probably in many other places, all the legal requirements are presented in the "boilerplate" part of the contract, where the standard legal obligations are stated. The contract is supplemented by other sections that specify the service purchased, the reporting requirements, and other issues of contractual matters. In the United States, the contract culture means that many contractual requirements are taken for granted. Contractual relationships imply legal language, exemplified in the boilerplate part of the contract. If contractual terms are violated, a whole range of instruments and legal passages can be invoked, and a

TABLE 9.3
The Contract Culture in the United States and Scandinavia

	United States	*Scandinavia*
Contract culture: rules and regulations	Mature	Developing
Contract culture: norms	Mature	Developing

court system exists to back up the claims. The local government laws relate to the state laws, which also have to take into account the federal legislation and new federal legislative initiatives.

In Scandinavia, the contract culture is not so well developed. Contractual relationships between purchasers and providers have not been institutionalized to the same degree as in the United States. That means that a lot of trial-and-error is going on in local governments. There is a great deal of insecurity as to what kind of legal requirements are binding. Consequently, local governments spend a lot of time finding out what kind of legislation to pay attention to and what kind of legislation can be observed less strictly. A primary source for this insecurity is the EU legislation. Most local governments and most providers of service complain that the EU legislation is too complicated to use in practice. Some criticism of complexity comes from the fact that still few tasks are contracted out in accordance with EU rules. The EU itself is in the process of changing the legislation for contracting out, but this brings even more insecurity in the short run because purchasers and providers unsure of the future rules are less committed to engaging in relationships here and now. Not many local governments in the EU buy their services from providers from other EU countries. There is still a huge cultural obstacle to a more competitive EU market for public services. We characterize the Scandinavian contract culture as a developing contract culture, which means that we would expect the Scandinavian—and the European—contract culture to have the potential to be as well developed as that of the United States at some point. The Scandinavian countries are going through a learning process that will educate purchasers, providers, and customers to become more like "contractual men."

THE FUTURE OF CONTRACTUAL GOVERNANCE

Contracting is not going to go away as a public policy issue. Governments seem to be always pressing for better, more efficient, and less costly services. Contracting is one tool to help achieve that goal. But the character of contracting may change. Contracting is likely to become more of a day-to-day question as policy evolves (Donahue 2000). Contracting still has a potential in many sectors, and new sectors are likely to become candidates for contracting purposes in the future (Domberger 1998). Contracting also seems to be spreading to more areas of the globe, as it has been a popular governance and management tool for thirty-odd years now (Hodge 2000).

Drawing from the analysis in this book, three types of challenges seem to be facing contracting in the future: First, contracting will be more sophisticated and develop more complex and contingent contractual models that will deal with new policy areas and more insights in conditions for employees and managers. Second, the provider profile will be more global in nature. There are already trends in this direction, which will change the contracting relationships in new fashions. Third, the overall governance structure of government will have to be more suited to a contract-based government. Previous fears of a "hollow" state have been followed by more complex models of governing and managing for public services in a contractualized institutionalized setting. This development put more emphasis on contractual design as a craft. The three challenges are explored in more detail in the following discussions.

More Sophisticated Contracting

Contracting is evolving into an art, a science, and a profession (to paraphrase Lynn [1996] on public management). Contracting is increasingly becoming an art, a function organizations have to do very well. Contracts are getting more and more refined. Contracts of local governments—like the contract from Dane County—cover many contingencies. There is room for negotiation, but there are also clearly defined sanctions and bodies that can settle contractual disputes if necessary. Contracting is also becoming more informed by theoretical contributions. Think, for example, of the influence of agency theory on the prospects of developing more refined contracts in the future. In negotiating contracts, both purchasers and providers have to think of transaction costs and who should bear the risks of covering them. The transaction costs are being measured more now than before, as governments try to estimate their full costs. In Scandinavia, the cost of preparing bids is still not counted fully into the cost definitions.

Finally, contracting is becoming a professional task in its own right. Lawyers have long profited from local governments' desire to contract out public services. Lawyers can act as consultants to both purchasers and providers. The complex EU competitive tender rules have provided work assignments for legal firms all over Europe. Even with a reformed EU set of rules on competitive tendering, the legal business is unlikely to be kept short of tasks to perform. The complexity of contracting requires more professional insight into the nature and implementation of contracts. As local governments do more contracting, they also will want to hire their own contracting staff. In many U.S. local governments, there are trained contract managers, who have job descriptions that focus on the process of contracting. In Scandinavia, the role of the contract manager in local governments is still developing. What local governments seem to have done is to pool resources on contracting expertise in specific offices in local government administration. Often these contract managers are close to the mayor and chief administrative officer because of the sensitivity of the contracting issue in many Scandinavian local governments.

More Prolific Providers

Providers are often local providers of public service to local governments. But increasingly providers are operating on a wider basis. This is in the nature of market development. Naturally, firms want to expand their market share and are looking for new markets. Providers have a varied profile, as the analysis has shown. There are big for-profit firms and small, local for-profit firms. There are big nonprofit organizations that operate on a national basis. And there are smaller nonprofit organizations, sometimes a single person in the human service area. In the future, it is likely that providers will be bigger and possess more dominant market positions. The example of Group 4 Falck as a global company has already been mentioned. But there are other examples. Such nonprofit organizations as Maximus Inc. in the United States have gained market shares in many American states. Organizations such as Maximus may be tempted to try to gain markets in other parts of the world at some point. In the waste management industry, American companies have already gained market shares in Scandinavia. Scandinavian companies are trying their luck in other Scandinavian countries. Some companies have a global outlook in their other operations not directed toward the public sector, for example, International Service Systems (ISS). There is no sign that these companies will gain a dominant market position in all global markets, but they can increasingly put local or national companies under pressure, thereby forcing more fierce global competition for public service delivery. Local and national companies cannot rest on their laurels anymore if they have secured contracts with local or national purchasers. They must be alert to the possibility of competition at any time. Eventually, the European market for public service delivery will become more competitive, forcing companies to take a European perspective on their operations. For purchasers, this means that they will combine their forces and go for bigger and better deals in the future, which will leave the local contract manager in a different position.

Governing Contracts in Different Cultural Settings

The third challenge is to think of contractual design in a more systematic manner. Much work has already been done in the literature on governing the hollow state (Milward and Provan 2000, for a summary of that debate). The challenge has been to maintain the ambition to govern in a setting where providers are diverse and have different profiles, such as nonprofit and for-profit firms mixed together on a local, national, and global basis. What kind of challenges do different cultural settings pose? The analysis in this book shows that contract culture is a factor to take into account. Purchasers and providers will have different expectations of the contracting process in different cultural settings. Purchasers and providers in U.S. local government will expect the legal requirements and the "hard" dimension of the contract to function well, and the challenge is to build relationships on top of that. Purchasers and providers in Scandinavian local government will expect to build informal relationships, but should be prepared to face the hard dimensions of the contract as well. Purchasers will have to be professional and will have to treat contracting as both an art and a science in all kinds of cultural settings. Providers will develop their product line, sometimes on a global scale or with more markets within their strategic reach, but will also, in some instances, have to conform to local or national institutional requirements. United States-dominated firms will have to have another policy toward employees if they operate in the Scandinavian countries. The contracting process, however, is getting more international in its profile. There is an increasing sharing of ideas and practices through organizations such as the OECD and the World Bank. Governments are learning public management practices, including how to contract out, from each other. It seems that the tide is turning toward a more international and global contracting process, which will pose new challenges for contractual management and governance.

Bibliography

Almquist, Roland. 2001. "Management by Contract: A Study of Programmatic and Technological Aspects." *Public Administration* 97 (3): 689–706.

Andersen, Kim Viborg, Carsten Greve, and Jacob Torfing. 1996. "Reorganizing the Danish Welfare State 1982–93." *Scandinavian Studies* 68: 161–187.

Behn, Robert D., and Peter A. Kant. 1999. "Strategies for Avoiding the Pitfalls of Performance Contracting." *Public Productivity and Management Review* 22 (4): 470–489.

Bertelsen, Christian. 2000. *Politikernes kontroldilemma*. Copenhagen: Akademisk.

Bjørn-Andersen, Mette. 2002. "Udliciteringsdebatten i Danmark: Er vi blevet klogere?" In Niels Ejersbo and Carsten Greve, eds., *Den offentlige sektor på kontrakt*. Copenhagen: Børsens Forlag, 35–49.

Boston, Jonathan, ed. 1995. *The State under Contract*. Wellington: Bridget Williams Books, 1995.

Boston, Jonathan, et al. 1996. *Public Management: The New Zealand Model*. Aukland: Oxford University Press.

Boston, Jonathan. 1999. "New Models of Public Management: The New Zealand Case." *Samfundsøkonomen* (5): 5–13.

Boyne, George. 1998. "Bureaucratic Theory Meets Reality: Public Choice and Service Contracting in U.S. Local Government." *Public Administration Review* 58 (6): 474–483.

Brewer, G., and Peter DeLeon. 1983. *The Foundations of Policy Analysis*. Pacific Grove, CA: Books/Cole.

Brixtofte, Peter. 2000. *Et opgør med 13 tabuer*. Viby J: JP Bøger.

Brown, Trevor L., and Matthew Potoski. 2003. "Contract Management Capacity in Municipal and County Governments." *Public Administration Review* 63 (2): 153–164.

Bryntse, Karin. 2000. *Kontraktsstyring i teori och praktik*. Lund: Lund Business Press.

Campbell, David, and Peter Vincent-Jones, eds. 1996. *Contracts and Economic Organisation: Socio-legal Initiatives*. Aldershot: Dartmouth.

Cassels, Mark. 2002. *How Governments Privatize. The Politics of Disvestment in the United States and Germany*. Washington, DC: Georgetown University Press.

Christensen, Tom, and Per Lægreid, eds. 2001. *New Public Management*. Ashbury: Ashgate.

Cohen, Steven. 2001."A Strategic Framework for Devolving Responsibility and Functions from Government to the Private Sector." *Public Administration Review* 61 (4): 432–440.

Collin, Sven-Erik. 1998. "In the Twilight Zone: A Survey of Public-Private Partnerships in Sweden." *Public Productivity and Management Review* 21 (3): 272–283.

Cooper, Phillip J. 2003. *Governing by Contract: Challenges and Opportunities for Public Managers*. Washington, DC: CQ Press.

Danish Ministry of Finance. 1995. *Værktøj til velfærd*. Copenhagen: Schultz.

Danish Ministry for Industry and Business. 1998. *Erhvervsredegørelse 1998*. Copenhagen: Schultz.

DeBruijn, H. 2002. *Managing Performance in the Public Sector*. London: Routledge.

DeHoog, Ruth Hoogland. 1984. *Contracting Out for Human Services*. Albany: State University of New York Press.

DeHoog, Ruth Hoogland. 1990. "Competition, Negotiation and Cooperation: Three Models for Service Contracting." *Administration and Society* 22 (3): 317–340.

DeLeon, Peter. 1999. "The Stages Approach to the Policy Process: What Has It Done? Where Is It Going?," In Paul A. Sabatier, *Theories of the Policy Process*. Boulder, CO: Westview Press.

Domberger, Simon. 1998. *The Contracting Organization*. Oxford: Oxford University Press.

Domberger, Simon, and Christine Hall. 1996. "Contracting for Public Services: A Review of Antipodean Experiences." *Public Administration* 74 (2): 129–147.

Donahue, John D. 2000. "How Far Can Privatization Go." In Robin Johnson and Norman Waltzer, eds., *Local Government Innovation* (pp. 253–266). Westport, CT: Quorum Books.

Drewry, Gavin. 2000. "The Citizen and the New Contractual Public Management: The Quest for New Forms of Accountability and a New Public Law." In Yvonne Fortin and Hugo van Hassel, eds., *Contracting in the New Public Management* (pp. 255–271). Amsterdam: IOS Press.

Eikås, Magne, and Per Selle. 2000. "A Contract Culture Even in Scandinavia: Makt- og demokratiutredning 1998–2003." *Rapportserien*, April (15).

Ejersbo, Niels, and Carsten Greve, eds. 2002. *Den offentlige sektor på kontrakt*. København: Børsens Forlag.

Flint, David. 1998. *Philosophy and Principles of Auditing*. London: Macmillan.

Fortin, Yvonne, and Hugo van Hassel, eds. 2000. *Contracting in the New Public Management*. Amsterdam: IOS Press.

Fountain, Jane. 2001. "Paradoxes of Public Service Customer Service." *Governance* 14 (1): 55–73.

Fromm, Johan, and E. Torsøe. 2000. Konkurrenseutstteing av bydelenes pleie- og omsorgstjeneste i Oslo - en sentraliseret og politiseret model. Oslo: Handelshøyskolen BI.

Gomard, Bernhard. *Almindelig kontraktret*. 1996. København: Jurist- og Økonomforbundets Forlag.

Greve, Carsten. 2000. "Exploring Contracts as Reinvented Institutions in the Danish Public Sector." *Public Administration* 78 (1): 153–164.

Greve, Carsten. 2003. "Public-Private Partnerships in Scandinavia." *International Public Management Review* 4 (2): 59–68.

Greve, Carsten and Niels Ejersbo. 2002. "Serial Organizational Monogamy: Building Trust into Contractual Relationships." *International Review of Public Administration* 7 (1): 39–51.

Hansen, Peter, Niels Ejersbo, and Olaf Rieper. 2000. *Målstyring i kommuner: To casestudier.* København: AKF-forlaget.

Harden, Ian. 1992. *The Contracting State.* Buckingham: Open University Press.

Harmon, Michael T., and Richard T. Mayer. 1986. *Organization Theory for Public Administration.* Glenview, IL: Scott, Foresman and Company.

Herbst, Douglas, and David Seader. 2000. "Providing Public Services through Long-Term Service Agreements." Robin A. Johnson and Norman Waltzer, eds. *Local Government Innovation* (pp. 105–122). Westport, CT: Quorum Books.

Hodge, Graeme A. 2000. *Privatization: An International Review of Performance.* Boulder, CO: Westview Press.

Hodge, Graeme A. 2002. "Who Steers the State When Governments Sign Public-Private Partnerships?" Paper for the American Society for Public Administration Conference, Phoenix, March.

Hood, Christopher. 1991. "A Public Management for All Seasons?" *Public Administration* 69: 3–19.

Hughes, Owen E. 1998. *Public Management and Administration: An Introduction,* 2d ed. London: Macmillan.

ICMA. 1999. *Contracting for Service Delivery: Local Government Choices.* Washington, DC: International City/County Management Association.

Institute of Public Policy Research. 2000. *Building Better Partnerships.* London: Institute of Public Policy Research.

ISS. 2002. Nye Mål - nye muligheder. Debat om offentlig-privat samarbejde. ISS: København.

James, Oliver. 1995. "Explaining the Next Steps in the Department of Social Security: The Bureau-Shaping Model of Central State Reorganisation." *Political Studies* 43 (4): 614–629.

Johnson, Robin A., and Norman Waltzer, eds. 2000. *Local Government Innovation: Issues and Trends in Privatization and Managed Competition.* Westport, CT: Quorum Books.

Kettl, Donald F. 1993. *Sharing Power: Public Governance and Private Markets.* Washington, DC: Brookings.

Kickert, Walther M. J., Erik-Hans Klijn, and Joop Koppenjan, eds. 1997. *Managing Complex Networks.* London: Sage.

Klausen, Kurt Klaudi, and Annick Magnier, eds. 1998. *The Anonymous Leader.* Odense: Odense University Press.

Kommunernes Landsforening (Konsulentvirksomhed for Økonomi og Ledelse). 2000. Udbud og udliciteringer i kommunerne. 6–21.

Lane, Jan-Erik. 2000. *New Public Management.* London: Routledge.

Light, Paul. 2000. *Making Non-Profits Work.* Washington, DC: Brookings.

Linder, Stephen. 1999. "Coming to Terms with Public-Private Partnerships." *American Behavioral Scientist,* 43 (1): 35–52.

Lynn, Laurence E. 1996. *Public Management as Art, Science and Profession.* Chatham, NJ: Chatham House.

March, James G., and Johan P. Olsen. 1989. *Rediscovering Institutions: The Organizational Basis of Politics.* New York: Free Press.

Martin, John. 1995. "Contracting and Accountability." In Jonathan Boston, ed., *The State under Contract* (pp. 78–111). Wellington: Bridget Williams Books.

Martin, Lawrence. 1999. *Determining a Level Playing Field for Public-Private Competition*. PriceWaterhouseCoopers Endowment for the Business of Government. Arlington, VA.

Martin, Lawrence. 1999. *Contracting for Service Delivery: Local Government Choices*. Washington, DC: ICMA.

Miller, Hugh, and James Simmons. 1998. "The Irony of Privatization." *Administration and Society* 35 (5): 513–532.

Milward, H. Brinton, and Keith G. Provan. 1998. "Principles for Controlling Agents: The Political Economy of Network Structure." *Journal of Public Administration Research and Theory* 8 (203): 221.

Milward, H. Brinton, and Keith G. Provan. 1993. "The Hollow State. Private Provision of Public Services" In Helen Ingram and Steven Rathgreb, eds., *Public Policy for Democracy* (pp. 222–237). Washington, DC: Brookings.

Milward, H. Brinton, and Keith G. Provan. 2000. "Governing the Hollow State." *Journal of Public Administration Research and Theory* 10 (2): 359–379.

Ministry of Business and Industry, Denmark. 1998. *Erhvervspolitisk redegørelse 1998*. Copenhagen: Schultz.

Ministry of Social Affairs, Denmark. 2000. *Socialpolitisk redegørelse*. Copenhagen, Ministry of Social Affairs, Denmark.

Mintzberg, Henry. 1983. *Structures in Fives*. Englewood Cliffs, NJ: Prentice-Hall.

Moe, Terry. 1984. "The New Economics of Organization." *American Journal of Political Science* 28: 739–777.

National Audit Office, Denmark. 1998. *Beretning om kontraktstyring*. Copenhagen: National Audit Office.

National League of Cities. 1997. *Municipal Service Delivery: Thinking through the Privatization Option*. Washington, DC: National League of Cities.

OECD. 1997. *Contracting Out Government Services: Best Practice Guidelines*. Paris: OECD.

Osborne, David, and Ted Gaebler. 1993 (1992). *Reinventing Government*. New york: Plume.

Osborne, Stephen, ed. 2000. *Public-Private Partnerships*. London: Routledge.

Pallesen, Thomas. 2000. "Udlicitering—den Paradoksale Kommunale Patologi." In Blom-Hansen et al., eds., *Kommunale Patologier*. Århus: Systime.

Pallot, June. 1999. "Central Government Innovation: The Case of New Zealand." Unpublished manuscript. Paper for Central Government Reform Workshop, Wissenscholl-Zentrum Berlin.

Peters, B. Guy. 1998. *Comparative Politics: Theory and Methods*. New York: New York University Press.

Pfiffner, Penn (Chair). 1997. *Promoting a More Competitive Government: A Report to the General Assembly by the Commission on Privatization*. Denver, CO: Department of Personnel/General Support Services.

Plovsing, Jan. 2000. *Dansk Socialpolitik*. København: Copenhagen Business School Publishing.

PLS Consult. 1997. *Erfaringer med udlicitering i kommuner og amter. Hovedrapport*. København: Schultz.

PLS Rambøll. 2000. *Kommunernes Administration i Konkurrence—intern kontraktstyring, udlicitering og partnerskab*. København: Schultz.

PLS Rambøll Management and concoursCepro. 2001. *Utvärdering av konkurrensutsättning inom Stokholms stad. Analys av process och effekter*. Stockholm: Schultz Grafisk A/S.

Pollitt, Christopher. 1995. "Justifications by Work or Faith? Evaluating the New Public Management." *Evaluation* 1 (2): 133–154.

Pollitt, Christopher. 2001. "Clarifying Convergence. Striking Similarities and Durable Differences in Public Management Reform." *Public Management Review* 3 (4): 471–492.

Pollitt, Christopher, and Geert Bouckaert. 2000. *Public Management Reform.* Oxford: Oxford University Press.

Power, Michael. 1994. *The Audit Explosion.* London: Demos.

Regeringen. 2002. Velfærd og valgfrihed. Copenhagen: Schultz.

Rhodes, R. A. W. 1997. *Understanding Governance.* Buckingham: Open University Press.

Roberts, Alasdair. 2001. "The Subscriber State." Paper for the ASPA Conference, Phoenix, Ariz. March.

Romzek, Barbara S. 1998. "Where the Buck Stops. Accountability in Reformed Public Organizations." In Patricia W. Ingraham, James R. Thompson, and Ronald P. Sanders, eds. *Transforming Government* (pp. 193–219). San Francisco: Jossey-Bass.

Romzek, Barbara S., and Jocelyn M. Johnston. 2000. "Reforming State Social Services through Contracting: Linking Implementation and Organizational Culture." In Jeffrey L. Brudney, Laurence O'Toole, and Hal G. Rainey, eds., *Advancing Public Management: New Developments in Theory, Methods* (pp. 173–195). Washington, DC: Georgetown University Press.

Romzek, Barbara, and Jocelyn M. Johnston. 2001. "State Contracting, Social Service Networks, and Effective Accountability: An Explanatory Model." Unpublished paper. Paper for presentation at the Annual Conference of the American Political Science Association.

Romzek, Barbara, S., and Jocelyn M. Johnston. 2002. "Effective Contract Implementation and Management: A Preliminary Model." *Journal of Public Administration Research and Theory* 12 (3): 423–453.

Røvik, Kjell Arne. 1998. *Moderne Organisasjoner.* Oslo: Fagbokforlaget.

Sabatier, Paul A. 1998. "The Advocacy Coalition Framework: Revisions and Relevance for Europe." *Journal of European Public Policy* 5 (1): 98–130.

Sabatier, Paul A., ed. 1999.*Theories of the Policy Process* (pp. 117–166). Boulder, CO: Westview Press.

Sabatier, Paul A., and Hank C. Jenkins-Smith. eds. 1993. *Policy Change and Learning: An Advocacy Coalition Approach.* Boulder, CO: Westview Press.

Sabatier, Paul A., and Hank C. Jenkins-Smith. 1999. "The Advocacy Coalition Framework: An Assessment." In Paul A. Sabatier, ed. *Theories of the Policy Process* (pp. 117–166). Boulder, CO: Westview Press.

Salamon, Lester. 1995. *Partners in Public Service.* Baltimore: Johns Hopkins University Press.

Savas, E. S. 1987. *Privatization: The Key to Better Government.* Chatham, NJ: Chatham House.

Savas, E. S. 2000. *Privatization and Public-Private Partnerships.* Chatham, NJ: Chatham House.

Savas, E. S. 2002. "Competiton and Choice in New York City Social Services." *Public Administration Review* 62 (1): 82–91.

Schick, Allen. 1996. *The Spirit of Reform.* Wellington: State Services Commission.

Scott, Graham. 1996. *Government Reform in New Zealand.* Washington, DC: World Bank.

Scott, W. Richard. 1995. *Institutions and Organizations.* London: Sage.

Selznick, Phillip. 1957/1984. *Leadership in Administration.* Berkeley: University of California Press.

Simon, Herbert. 1976 (1945). *Administrative Behaviour.* New York: Free Press.

Sizer, Ed. 2000. "Impact on Public Organizational Structure and Behaviour: Managed Competition and Privatization." In Robin A. Johnson and Norman Waltzer, eds., *Local Government Innovation* (pp. 210–235). Westport, CT: Quorum Books.

Taylor-Gooby, Peter. 1998. *Choice and Public Policy.* London: Macmillan.

Terry, Larry. 1998. "Administrative Leadership, Neo-Managerialism, and the Public Management Movement." *Public Administration Review* 58 (3): 194–200.

Truett, Lila, and Dale Truett. 1984. *Intermediate Microeconomics.* St. Paul, MN: West.

Van Ham, Hans, and Joop Koppenjan. 2001. "Building Public-Private Partnerships: Assessing and Managing Risk in Port Development." *Public Management Review* 3 (4): 593–616.

Vincent-Jones, Peter. 1999. "Competition and Contracting in the Transition from CCT to Best Value: Towards a More Reflexive Regulation?" *Public Administration* 77 (2): 273–291.

Wallin, B. 1997. "The Need for a Privatization Process: Lessons from Development and Implementation." *Public Administration Review* 57 (1): 11–20.

Walsh, Kieron. 1995. *Public Services and Market Mechanisms.* London: Macmillan.

Warner, Milred. 2000. "Structuring the Market for Services Delivery: A New Role for Local Government." In Robin A. Johnson and Norman Walzer, eds., *Local Government Innovation* (pp. 85–104). Wesport, CT: Quorum.

Wegener, Alexander. 1998. "Evaluating Competitively Tendered Contracts." *Evaluation* 4 (2): 189–203.

Wegener, Alexander. 2000. *Wettbewerb in der Kommunalverwaltung: Ein Vergleich kommunaler Wettbewerbsansätze in den USA, Grossbritannien und Neuseeland.* Dissertation. Institut für Politizwissenschaft der Fern Universitât Hagen.

Williamson, Oliver E. 1975. *Markets and Hierarchies: Analysis and Antitrust Implications.* New York: Free Press.

Williamson, Oliver E. 1979. "Transaction-cost Economics: The Governance of Contractual Relations." *Journal of Law and Economics* 22: 233–262.

Williamson, Oliver E. 1985. *The Economic Institutions of Capitalism.* New York: Free Press.

Williamson, Oliver E. 1996. *The Mechanisms of Governance.* Oxford: Oxford University Press.

Winter, Søren. 1994. *Implementering.* Aarhus: Systime.

Wolf, Adam. 2000. "Tendenser og temaer i forvaltningspolitikken."*Nordisk Administrativt Tidsskrift* 81 (4): 368378.

Yeatman, Anne. 1995. "Interpreting Contemporary Contractualism." In Jonathan Boston, ed., *The State under Contract* (pp. 124–139). Wellington: Bridget Williams Books.

Yin, Robesrt K. 1989. *Case Study Research.* Newbury Park, CA: Sage.

Index

About the Authors

CARSTEN GREVE, Ph.D., is associate professor in public management at the Department of Political Science, University of Copenhagen, Denmark. His research is concentrated on public management and governance, with special emphasis on contracting and public-private partnerships. He has published his work in journals such as *Public Management Review, Governance,* and *Public Administration.*

NIELS EJERSBO, Ph.D., is associate professor and department chair in public management at the University of Southern Denmark. His research has primarily been focused on local government and organization, with recent emphasis on contracting. He has published articles in the United States and internationally.